Systematic Analysis

Harley H. Hinrichs/Graeme M. Taylor

A Primer on Benefit–Cost Analysis
and Program Evaluation

Goodyear Publishing Company, Inc.
Pacific Palisades, California

Copyright 1972 © by
GOODYEAR PUBLISHING COMPANY, INC.
Pacific Palisades, California

All rights reserved. No part of this book may be reproduced
in any form or by any means without permission in writing
from the publisher.

Library of Congress Catalog Card Number: 76-188961

ISBN: 0-87620-881-2

Y-8812-3

Current Printing (Last Number): 10 9 8 7 6 5 4 3 2 1

Printed in the United States of America

Contents

Preface

A new generation of systematic analysis and analysts is here. The sixties witnessed the revolution of "Planning, Programming, Budgeting Systems": the greatly expanded use of PPB at federal, state, and local levels, as well as some of its more egregious goofs. The seventies will be more sophisticated. Analytic techniques have been reformed. Much of the early mystique has been demythologized. This "second generation" of analysis has tried to cut away much of the bureaucratic rigamarole of the earlier formalized systems so that the inner core of systematic analysis—really hard organized thinking—survives to tackle real problems.

This book simplifies and summarizes the core of this new generation of systematic analysis. It does so in a "how to" and "how was done" fashion. A concise but hopefully incisive primer outlines the skeletal theoretical framework for the analyst. Once this stage is set, Part II presents actual case studies of analysis, both of problems and of solutions. Part III provides "successful" examples of completed analysis, illustrating different types of analysis. An Appendix provides notes on planning, analysis, and evaluation.

This book follows and complements our *Program Budgeting and Benefit-Cost Analysis Cases, Text and Readings* (Goodyear Publishing Company, 1969). This first "case book" was not only adopted by many colleges, universities, institutes, and government units but it became the official text in U.S. Civil Service Commission courses for federal middle-management trainees. However, the demand arose for a shorter primer version—especially one wherein not only cases would be presented but also follow-up analyses and some attached solutions. Thus, *Systematic Analysis* came into existence, but this book can also stand alone or as a supplement to other books in the field. And our first "case book" can still serve its purpose of providing a broad range of text, readings, and cases (without conclusions so as to enhance their classroom use) whereas this new book can satisfy the student or official with less time and/or with greater curiosity to see both "how to" and "how it was done." Both books can be used in tandem so the student may take the lessons from the more recent completed cases and re-apply them to the "unfinished" cases of the first book. Or, for certain courses with limited weeks for analysis of decision making in the public sector, this book will suffice.

As a primer on systematic analysis, this book will be useful to undergraduate and graduate students in economics, public administration, business administration, and government in their courses partly or solely concerned with the public sector, government decision making, public finance and expenditures, investment criteria, urban problems, public policy issues, government and business, public administration, and so on. In addition, government officials, trainees, executives, and planners will find this primer to be a valuable part of their libraries.

The book focuses in capsule form on many "quality of life" issues that are becoming more important in the seventies: educating the mentally retarded, recreation opportunities for inner city neighborhoods, services to the children handicapped in their first eight years, the nature of justice and reducing court delays, and the "blindness system." However, certain more traditional examples of analysis are also included to give the student "hard" discipline in using analytical tools: these cases include deploying fire boats in New York harbor, small-site industrial renewal programs, and cost-effectiveness analysis of bombs versus missiles for the Air Force.

Acknowledgments are due to many. We are indebted to our students at the University of Maryland Graduate School (most being federal management trainees) for feeding back to us comments on some of the analyses and cases. We also thank various faculty colleagues and seminar attendants who were exposed to these ideas in our various visits to Harvard, Wisconsin, Yale, the U.S. Naval Academy, The George Washington University, and elsewhere. We are grateful for the logistical and inspirational support of Management Analysis Center, Inc., both in Cambridge and Washington, for providing source material and editorial guidance. Our research assistants and secretaries who helped on the manuscript deserve many thanks for their dedication: Joan Henderson, Sherri Wahle, and Elaine Chastain.

HARLEY H. HINRICHS
GRAEME M. TAYLOR

Part One: The Theory of Systematic Analysis

The Theory of Systematic Analysis

INTRODUCTION

Improving the quality of life and the quantities of goods and services available for consumption now and in the future depends on two factors: resources and decisions as to how resources are used. We are often stuck with the former. The latter we can affect if not always control. This introduction,[1] which summarizes systematic analysis, deals with improving decision making in the public (government) sector.

Systematic analysis is nothing less, or more, than the organized application of rational thought to the solutions of allocation problems. It assumes a world of hedonists rather than masochists, that people in general like more better than less, that they prefer pleasure to pain, and that they want solutions to their problems.

Systematic analysis has appeared at different times and places under various disguises and names, many referring to variations on an overall theme. These names include investment analysis, payout analysis, rate of return analysis, operations or systems analysis, benefit-cost analysis, cost-effectiveness analysis, and economic analysis. Here we use the term "systematic analysis."

Problems are seen either as type I: maximize benefits, given a fixed budget, or type II: minimize costs, given fixed objectives. Of course, interesting insights can be gained when either or both benefits or costs are varied slightly (type III problems) to indicate marginal benefits and costs, but ultimately problems can be transformed into type I or II.

This introduction is primarily a survey of the basic categories of systematic analysis. The categories are: (1) objectives (2) constraints (3) externalities (4) time (the interest rate choice) and (5) risk and uncertainty. How these categories or conceptual boxes are filled determines whether or not the analysis will be useful to the decision maker.

---

1. This paper was prepared by Harley H. Hinrichs. It stands on the shoulders of the following earlier contributions which, in a more detailed fashion, synthesized, summarized, and simplified systematic analysis: Otto Eckstein, "A Survey of the Theory of Public Expenditure Criteria," in *Public Finances: Needs, Sources, and Utilization,* National Bureau of Economic Research (Princeton University Press, 1961), pp. 439–494; A. R. Prest and R. Turvey, "Cost-Benefit Analysis: A Survey," *Economic Journal,* December 1965, pp. 683–735; and Harley H. Hinrichs, "Government Decision Making and the Theory of Benefit-Cost Analysis: A Primer," in *Program Budgeting and Benefit-Cost Analysis: Cases, Text and Readings,* Harley H. Hinrichs and Graeme M. Taylor, eds. (Pacific Palisades, Cal.: Goodyear Publishing Co., 1969). Discussions with Charles L. Schultze and a detailed criticism of the original manuscript by Robert H. Haveman and Graeme M. Taylor also contributed in a major way to this introduction; the author is indebted to these individuals. However, all shortcomings are the sole property of the author.

However, this skeletonlike outline of systematic analysis is first preceded by a discussion of the distinguishing characteristics of *government* decision making, its process and measurement problems, as contrasted to private-sector decision making.

I. THE GOVERNMENT AS DECISION MAKER

Decisions and their necessity reflect the scarce nature of things. Because one cannot have everything simultaneously, one must pick and choose. In theorizing about the private sector, this picking and choosing is often put in terms of simple models whereby consumer satisfaction and producer profits are to be maximized. It is often a world where both inputs and outputs are chosen and priced under conditions of free competition.

There are three primary differences between government and private decision making: the nature of the process, the nature of the goods, and the nature of the goals. We examine each in detail.

1. *The nature of decision making* in the public sector *is a group process.* It involves interactions, pressures, and bargains among differing groups from the electorate to executive and legislative organs. There is no one single consumer or producer whose welfare or profit is to be maximized. Thus the process of decision making itself becomes an important variable. What problems are chosen, who decides the solutions, how decisions are communicated, what incentives are developed to enforce decisions, what concessions made in one decision affect other problem and solution choices—all these questions take on added importance in public sector decision making.

2. *The nature of goods* involved in public sector decisions is often quite different from those in private decisions. Goods may be divided into three categories:

• *Specific goods* are finite, exhaustible, and exclusive in that the person who owns the good can exclude others from its benefits; likewise, the consumption of the good, such as food, is limited to one person at one time. Thus, prices can allocate.

• *Collective goods* (often called "public goods") are available for consumption by all and from which none can be excluded, such as nuclear defense or television broadcasting (assuming everyone has access to a TV set and no picture scrambling devices are used). Thus, prices cannot allocate.

• *Quasi-collective goods* are specific goods with significant collective externalities. They could be produced and sold on a specific basis, such as elementary education, but the spillover effects to general society are so great that society may take over their production to provide a greater quantity at a lower price than would be provided by private producers selling to private consumers.

Although both the private and public sector may deal in all three types of goods (see Fig. 1), the public sector is primarily concerned with collective and quasi-collective goods (defense, education, welfare, transportation, recreation) whereas the private sector is primarily concerned with specific consumption

Figure 1
Goods and Decisions: Public and Private

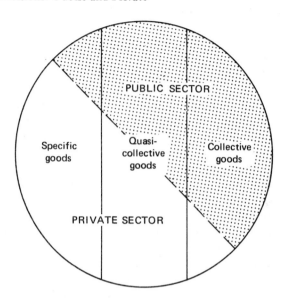

goods. As the nature of such goods differ, so do the decision-making rules for their pricing and optimal allocation.

3. *The nature of goals* is substantially different in the public and private sectors. Government goals—that is, goals for a group—are often highly complex, rapidly changing, and far more difficult to know and measure than those in the standard models of private decision making which focus on maximizing individual profits or consumption satisfaction. Group goals may involve a "netting out" of benefits and costs among its members in order to arrive at decisions. When an individual decides, he may gain or lose; he acts to gain. When a group decides, some of its members may gain or lose more than others; the incidence of such pluses and minuses may determine if the group acts.

In the broader constitutional sense, the range of public sector values and goals goes far beyond the private sector's goals of goods to consume and profits to be made. They include purposes to "form a more perfect union, establish justice, insure domestic tranquility, provide for the common defense, promote the general welfare, and secure the blessing of liberty upon ourselves and our posterity." These outstrip the simple dollar yardsticks and computer quantifications applied in private sector decision making.

In a narrower sense the public sector has goals for the economy which include influencing the allocation of resources, stabilizing prices and employment (at a "maximum" level), "improving" the distribution of income, affecting national economic growth rates, and conserving national resources including a livable environment.

As these and other public goals change, conflict, and involve complex interrelationships, the job of public decision making takes on a character different from that in the private sector.

Given these three major characteristics which distinguish public from private decision making, let us now turn to the decision-making process in government itself and then examine the essential framework for systematic analysis.

II. THE DECISION-MAKING PROCESS

The world of systematic analysis is one of scarce means to achieve unlimited ends. The process of decision making in such a world is to (1) convert these end values into objectives, or quantified desired outputs, that can be measured or ranked in priority, and (2) convert the scarce means into alternative sets of predictable outcomes, or output possibilities, that best correspond to the objectives set.

The prime difficulty in decision making as a process is the lack of correspondence between ends and means. Teachers (means) are not the same as better-educated children (ends). More miles of paved road (means) are not the same as greater ease and speed in moving among geographical points (ends). Such incommensurabilities plague the decision-making process. The job, then, is to attempt a "double conversion" of values into objectives (outputs) and inputs into predictable outputs. Then the decision is easy to make: A is better than B because A is bigger than B. When values and inputs, ends and means, can be put into the same common denominator of outputs, then comparisons can be made and decisions become obvious.

For example, society values education; society has resources, say in terms of a Type I problem, fixed budgetary resources. The job for the decision maker is to convert the "value" of education into a set of ranked outputs, or in this example, high-school graduates in a school district. Likewise, the budgetary funds (inputs) may be transformed into differing numbers of high-school graduates depending on the different allocations made of the funds: so many dollars into buildings, training aids, books, teachers, supervisory personnel, counselors, etc. Each combination of inputs—given technologically researched and known production possibilities—would result in some output: a number of high-school graduates. The job of picking the "best set" of inputs is then obvious (the one that maximizes high-school graduates). However, as should also be obvious, the difficulty is not in making the decision after the "double conversion" is made. The crux of the problem is in the conversion itself: finding agreement on an agreed set of outputs desired by the value system in the community and discovering the technological outcomes of using different sets of inputs.

In brief, then, the decision-making process involves: (1) converting values into objectives, or deciding more precisely what is really wanted in operational, measurable terms (2) discovering the range of alternatives whereby these objectives may be accomplished, or converting a storehouse of resources into differing combinations to reach outputs (3) recognizing which of these alternative strategies are not feasible (the role of constraints) and, finally, (4) making the decision itself.

Such a process often requires the construction of a "model." If one is to compare the extent to which each alternative set of inputs contributes to the achievement of the objective, one needs a framework. A good model explains exactly what the relationships are, not merely that such relationships exist. The value of such a model is that it is explicit: it can be studied, criticized, evaluated, and improved. For public policy issues, this is especially important. The public needs to know how its values and votes are being translated into operational objectives. It also needs to know the route chosen for reaching that objective, alternative routes that have been rejected and, indeed, other objectives that might have to be given up for the sake of reaching the original objective.

In a sense, only when "costs" are translated into "objectives foregone" can the people of the community make enlightened decisions. Even then, the decisions may be fraught with incommensurabilities. A society may desire both defense and education. Given limited resources, choices become complex; one must know, for example, not only the predictable outcomes (education) of a Headstart program or another aircraft carrier (defense) but also whether or not one can evaluate an extra aircraft carrier as "costing" two Headstart programs (cross-budgetary trade-offs).

In theory this process is simple; it is difficult only in practice. In theory, say in a world of no time, no space, no uncertainties, one merely decides what he wants. He specifies his ends or objectives. He measures them or quantifies benefits. Then he uses his limited means, after scanning the range of possible outcomes of using the inputs in different combinations, to achieve the greatest possible value of his wants (benefits).

In such a decision-making process, three types of problems arise. In problem type I the decision maker is confronted with a certain or fixed budget so that his task is to maximize benefits obtainable from this budget. An oversimplified example of such a constrained budget problem would be the choice of the optimum mix of transportation facilities to handle the traffic demand between Washington, D. C. and New York City, given a budget of $4 billion. Or even more simple, building the highest pyramid with a given number of bricks.

In problem type II the decision maker is required to minimize costs to achieve a given specified level of benefits (outputs). This type of problem is often called "cost-effectiveness" analysis and is typically used by the Department of Defense. Millenia ago this might have required finding the least number of bricks to build a pyramid 100 meters high. Today it might involve finding the "least cost" mix of land- and sea-based missiles and/or aircraft to present a credible "second strike" capability.

Type III problems are the most difficult of the three because both benefits and costs (ends and means) can be treated as variables. Consequently, a competent evaluation requires an analysis of the optimal size and design of each of the alternative possibilities, the measurement of the costs and benefits of each, and then a choice among them. A typical "macro" style problem is the President's decision as to both the size and shape of the total federal budget.

Here the solutions, in theory at least, are twofold. (1) One ultimately must make some valuation of the marginal benefits of resources used in the private and public sectors, the cost of transferring resources from one sector to the other, and the likely outcomes of decisions to make such transfers. In theory one would wish to equate the marginal benefits of resource use in both sectors, thus solving for the optimal size of the public sector; once this is done, the problem reverts to that of type I, fixed budget, maximize benefits. (2) More operationally, one may focus on how sensitive benefits are to small or marginal changes in inputs and vice versa. This process of "sensitivity analysis" provides useful information so that the analyst may then juggle the sizes of different programs until each dollar input at the margin yields the same return. That is, he juggles inputs and outputs until he no longer is able to increase the total pot of benefits.

The decision maker, if he wants "good" decisions, implicitly must feel and explicitly must ask five questions.

1. What is wanted? What is an explicit and measurable statement of objectives? (*Specify ends.*)
2. How does one know if he gets what he wants? How are the benefits (in terms of attaining the objectives) to be quantified and measured? (*Quantify ends.*)
3. What does it cost? Which costs are to be included and how are such costs of attaining the objectives to be quantified and measured to allow their comparison with the benefits? (*Specify and quantify means.*) Ultimately, such costs are other objectives foregone.
4. What are the constraints within which the decision must be made? What alternatives are excluded because of these constraints? Can such initial constraints (such as budget size, legal blocs, technological limits) be varied? (*Specify constraints.*)
5. What are the side effects or spillover effects from the decision? Are such externalities—not counted in the model's tabulation of costs and benefits—of sufficient importance to modify the final decision? (*Consider side effects.*)

The Problem of Measurement

This decision-making sequence is based on comparison of costs and benefits. And the crux of comparison is measurement with the same yardstick. Accurate comparisons for both private and public decisions, therefore, require the valuing of outputs and inputs in the same unit of account.

Unfortunately, the problem of assigning values to the outputs and inputs of public programs is more difficult than for business or household decisions. Much difficulty in public decisions occurs because many of the outputs and inputs of public undertakings accrue to and are contributed by a number of entities, not just one as in the case of personal or business decisions. When a businessman contemplates an investment decision, he worries only about the revenues which the investment will bring into his firm and compares these revenues only with the cost of the investment to his firm. The public decision maker, on the other hand, must be concerned with the values placed on the program's outputs by each of the recipients of the output of the public program and with the value of the costs incurred by each citizen who is forced to sacrifice something to support the undertaking.

For example, in valuing the outputs of a labor retraining program, the public decision maker must be concerned not only with the added productivity of the workers but also with the benefits that society reaps because of the changed behavior of the newly trained people. Among other things, trainees might be less likely to be involved in criminal or other antisocial behavior and more likely to provide stable homes and better education for their children. These outputs, both positive and negative, have value and would be considered by the public decision maker in evaluating alternatives.

Similarly, the inputs to (or costs of) a public program are sometimes exceedingly difficult to value. The labor-retraining program, for example, is paid for by taxes. In paying taxes, citizens are forced to cut back on private consumption and investment. These foregone opportunities represent the value of the inputs to the public program. Again, the valuing problem appears more difficult for public than for private decision makers.

Using Market or Shadow Prices as Public Yardsticks

A market economy contains an enormous and automatic information gathering system. It performs an important social function by placing value on every good, service, input, and output which passes through a market. This value or price has a highly significant characteristic. It represents the combined judgment of a large number of people involved in both producing and consuming the good or service; the worth of the last unit exchanged is the index.

Because this information gathering system exists, one may say, "When the government buys $1 million of steel, the people of a society are being forced to give up $1 million worth of things which they would otherwise have purchased and enjoyed. The cost to the society of the government's spending is, therefore, $1 million.

"Flood control project X will, it is estimated, prevent flood damages of an average of $500,000 per year. The benefit to society of building the project is equal to the satisfaction which the people of the society would experience by having an additional $500,000 a year to spend as they wished."

Even when the outputs of government programs do not themselves pass over a market, observed market prices which approximate the value of the nonmarketed government outputs are often available. For example, even though the services of the national parks are not sold, there are analagous recreation facilities which give some basis for valuing the output of parks. Moreover, other characteristics of economic behavior can be used to estimate the value to people of national parks. Expenditures of people traveling to and from recreation sites have been used with some success in estimating the value placed on recreation.

However, in making this strong claim for the helpfulness of "valued" outputs and inputs of public programs, a few warnings should be offered. First, while market prices do provide guidance in valuing public program outputs and inputs, some market prices are notoriously distorted and must themselves be adjusted. Where monopoly power is present, observed prices are likely to be "too high." Likewise, the money wage for labor is too high if the laborer would otherwise be unemployed. Furthermore, prices fail to have normative significance if the buyers and sellers operate without adequate information. Similarly, labor immobility and unaccounted-for "externalities"—or side effects in the private sector—cause observed market prices to lose their significance. Where such conditions are present, the securing of the observed market prices is only the beginning of the task. If they are to be correctly used, they must be adjusted to compensate for these imperfections.

Second, all prices, even those produced in a perfect market economy, depend on prevailing consumer tastes and preferences. One may question the legitimacy of these preferences or values as a guide for social policy. Are we to accept tastes that favor automobile gadgetry rather than increased auto safety or tastes that prefer increased drug use regardless of social cost? The consumer may be sovereign but his legislators can rule for social good rather than for private values. Thus, in certain cases where there is a clear wedge between private and social costs or when market prices are grossly imperfect, the analyst may use his own set of prices for inputs and outputs. This process of adjusting faulty market signals is called "shadow pricing."

In some instances there is no choice other than to use such prices. Within the federal government itself goods transferred from one agency to another may have no comparable market value. For example, transferring secondhand Sherman tanks from the U.S. Army in Germany to the military assistance program in Turkey requires the use of some set of "internal prices." Thus, a cost-effectiveness study of military assistance to Turkey would hinge to some degree on the appropriateness of different bookkeeping prices charged for military hardware in the program. A different mix of hardware would result if the internal prices were based on the historical value measure "cost less depreciation" rather than on "replacement cost," "marginal utility," or "cost of alternative weapons substitutes."

In other instances, "shadow pricing" may be required as well. Foreign exchange rates may be arbitrarily fixed; labor or capital may have no alternative uses;

monopoly or monopsonistic pricing may exist; government taxes, subsidies, or regulations may distort market prices and even temporary market fluctuations may not reflect future price levels relevant to the life of a government program. Thus, while there is usually a strong *prima facie* case for market prices, the analyst may wish to check his original analysis by substituting shadow prices in such instances.

III. OBJECTIVES

The problem of stating explicitly the objectives of public undertakings is no smaller than determining a way to define and measure social welfare. Ultimately, one must ask: What does society want? What does society value most highly? In principle, these questions are answered by stating that society should maximize the welfare of its people. (But even here there is the question raised by Edmund Burke of the people yet unborn and those long dead.) In fact, all lesser ends may be considered to be merely means toward this ultimate end.

The problem, of course, is to attach numerical values, which this ultimate end (if indeed it is) and all other "lesser" ends make toward its achievement. Even if one could quantify this ultimate goal or, as economists have done, at least get some "ordinal" feel for the shape of the contours of such a welfare mountain, most decision makers deal with lesser ends. (The "ordinal" welfare approach is based on ranking preferences without attaching absolute values to desired ends as in the "cardinal" approach.) Among the practitioners of systematic analysis, the following conventions have been widely adopted as a way to specify and quantify social welfare gains and losses. There are four choices.

1. Ignore societies, groups, regions; attach value only to individuals (thus junking organic theories of the state), and maximize.

$$W = W(W_1, \ldots, W_n) \ \ (W = \text{welfare})$$

Thus, given this maximand, there remain three other questions for any policy decision to change the status quo, and therefore move toward maximizing welfare,[2] a change in welfare being:

$$\Delta W = W(\Delta W_1, \ldots, \Delta W_n)$$

2. Play the game "Everybody Wins." That is, move the pieces in the game of life so that all individuals gain in welfare, i.e., $\Delta W_i > 0$ for all i (i = individual).

2. Welfare as used in this paper should not be confused with welfare as used in the expression "health, education and welfare" or "social welfare work." It is restricted to the more technical economist's definition concerned with individual's subjective sense of satisfaction and/or the achievement of individual preferences.

3. Play the game "Somebody Wins, Nobody Loses" (movement toward Pareto optimality). That is, move the pieces so that at least one individual gains and nobody is worse off, i.e., $\Delta W_i \geqslant 0$ for all i.

4. Play the game "The Winners Outweigh the Losers." That is, move the pieces so that there is a *net* gain; the gains outweighing the losses. This results in a further decision being required. Do you measure at prices before the move (Kaldor), after the move (Hicks), or both (Scitovsky)?

Even after these four relatively easy decisions are made, one must find proxies for "welfare." Do we choose as the appropriate stand-in term "income," "consumption," "probable income or consumption," "probable present (or terminal) value of a future stream of income and/or consumption"?

The game most economists and policy makers prefer seems to be game 4, such as in the Trade Expansion Act of 1962, whereby the gains to the winners (consumers and exporters) are considered to outweigh the losses to the losers (import-substitute industries and their workers) with compensation—adjustment assistance—to be made in theory if not in practice.[3] The proxy most often used for welfare seems to be per capita income, or in more sophisticated analyses, the present value of an expected future stream of income for the individuals affected by a policy decision (for example farmers affected by an irrigation project). Secondary benefits (e.g. pecuniary spillovers or windfall profits) are generally excluded. For example, the benefits of irrigation projects may be determined by computing the value of the increase in grain output (less increased farmers' costs) but would exclude the increased profits of the railroads in hauling the grain.

Criteria Other Than "Maximizing the Present Value of Society's Income"

When uncertainties and incommensurabilities exist, one may have to rely on objectives or criteria quite different from the conventional "maximum per capita income" variety. For example, in a series of possible outcomes, one may wish to opt for a *maximin* criterion: maximize the minimum possible gain regardless of what moves you or others may make. In U.S. defense strategy the choice of offensive and defensive weapons quite often is premised on achieving some "assured destructive capability" (or minimum effective deterrent) rather than, say, maximizing social welfare.

In other cases, one may choose a *minimax* criterion: minimize the maximum possible loss regardless of what moves you or others may make. In U.S. civil defense, expenditures may be allocated on the basis of preserving a functioning government and in minimizing loss of lives and property. Infantry tactics, for example, are often based on the enemy's capabilities rather than on his suspected

3. See Harley H. Hinrichs, "A Benefit-Cost Analysis of the Removal of Import Quotas on the Stainless Steel Flatware Industry." *Hearings* (Washington, D.C.: U.S. Tariff Commission, May 23, 1967).

intentions as a way to minimize loss to your own forces in case you guessed wrongly about his intentions. There are a host of other possible objectives or criteria one may use for preventing riots or for reducing flood damage. The major point here is that to have defined the objective is the critical first step in making a rational decision.

Pitfalls in Setting Objectives

Because stating objectives and measuring outputs are so critical in the decision-making process, let us examine five common types of errors: (1) regarding means as ends (2) not regarding means as ends (3) being biased toward the quantifiable (4) forgetting that one objective may be *not* to reveal objectives and (5) having multiple objectives.

1. *Regarding means as ends:* Obviously, one cannot use "the" ultimate end of social welfare or satisfaction for the analysis of every issue. One is almost always involved in choosing a penultimate or prior "end," which is one of the means to a further end. How far back should one go in selecting "ends" or objectives for a particular area? In education, for example, one may achieve distorted results if one substitutes proxies such as teacher/pupil ratios or classroom space per pupil or teachers' salaries—which are only means to an end—for "maximizing education per dollar spent" or, more suboptimally, admissions to advanced schools, high exam scores, or increased lifetime earnings. Obviously, we may be quite uncertain whether the attainment of some proxy "means" will lead to the accomplishment of either a more ultimate social welfare end or some immediate suboptimal target.

Likewise, in foreign aid programs, the end is not necessarily to increase investment or inputs (such as fertilizer) but to increase investments only in as much as they produce outputs (such as food).

2. *Not regarding means as ends:* Paradoxical with the first error of focusing on means as ends, a second error is *not* to consider a means an end when indeed it is. In many areas of life, the means is highly valued in and of itself. Justice and politics supply the foremost examples. "Effective" law is not a legal system that fills the jails or maximizes convictions per dollar or maximizes fines per conviction; it is, rather, a system which guarantees "due process" wherein rights are preserved. In court, the jurors may not have a specific way of knowing whether a man is guilty or innocent, right or wrong; they can only say that the decision was reached in accordance with the previously adopted consensus as to how such decisions are to be made. Likewise in the political arena, the means toward reaching group decisions through democratic processes—free assembly, free speech, voting rights, and so on—may be valued as more important than the outcome itself. Thus, the student of government decision making has to determine if the decision process is a more valued end than the decisions themselves.

3. *Being biased toward the quantifiable: To measure is to know but not*

necessarily the right thing. Quantification, as a process in and of itself, is at the very core of science. However, improperly used it can lead to distorted results in the art and science of government decision making. All decision-making models must simplify; a one-to-one map is of no use. But it is here that the danger lurks. The science part of the decision making has a built-in and justified bias toward including these variables (both means and ends) which can be quantified. This bias is all to the good unless the excluded nonquantifiable variables do in fact make a difference; if the critical means or ends are nonquantified or nonquantifiable, then superficial precision with numbers within the analysis may be irrelevant to the solution. Indeed, many ends—beauty, love, freedom, justice, wisdom—may be obscured by a myopic fetishlike preoccupation with first-glance numbers.

4. *Forgetting that one objective may be not to reveal objectives.* At some times and in some places, certain political coalitions or ideologically fragmented groups cannot spell out precise objectives or even agree on objectives. Passing an education bill in the Congress involves different groups with different motives. Preventing national or even world civil wars may obscure changing or changeable objectives. Pragmatism may take precedence over ideological motives if jobs are to be done. Thus, the student of government decision making must not assume that obscure and obfuscated objectives are totally without function. Many times objectives are uncertain, changing, conflicting; this apparent confusion may not be the signal for total inaction but instead for discovering and discussing objectives in the very process of moving in a general direction. Objectives often are a result of a feed-back process in getting the job under way and in working toward broader goals.

5. *Having multiple objectives, a dilemma:* When the objective is not simply maximizing one objective (such as per capita income) but instead consists of a series of objectives and their distribution among individuals within a society, then the problem becomes sticky. The problem is no longer economic efficiency in small terms but economic allocation as political economy with income distribution as one of the objectives. Thus, in a much broader context, one may have to place different "weights" on dollars received from low-income individuals as contrasted to more wealthy individuals. A high benefit-cost ratio on a bridge connecting two wealthy suburbs and financed by general sales tax revenues may not be directly comparable to a lower benefit-cost ratio on a bridge between two poor communities financed by a progressive income tax.

In other instances, procedures for evaluating benefits and costs of public programs become highly complex when the social value of dollars to various groups of people or regions within a country can no longer be assumed to be equal. Judgments made by the political system may be necessary to ascertain how much of one objective (say economic growth) may be sacrificed in return for the increased attainment of another objective (say social stability, income distribution, national pride or political harmony). However, even in the absence in such a political determination, the analyst can offer a range of assumptions as to potential trade-offs so political judgments can be made on the basis of explicit costs rather than pure intuition.

IV. CONSTRAINTS

Having settled upon some set of objectives, the next logical step is to determine what limits their achievement. In the broadest sense, limited resources are the prime constraint. This "economic" aspect of the problem requires allocating finite resources so as to achieve the maximum objective or an array of objectives. In addition to this most basic constraint, there are a bundle of other circumstances which obstruct the attainment of an objective. Indeed, for each decision, either public or private, there are likely to exist constraints in addition to the resource limitation. These additional constraints are physical, legal, administrative, distributional, political, and financial.

Physical constraints—to produce an output, inputs must pass through a process of production. This production process, even if it is the most modern and efficient available, can only utilize given technology and knowledge.

Legal constraints—laws, property rights, international conventions, agency rulings, and so on can reduce any list of feasible solutions. In fact, legal constraints often inhibit (if not prohibit) sound economic analysis of public expenditure decisions. For example, until recently, administrative procedure required that an inappropriately low interest rate be used to place the future benefits and costs of federal water resource projects on a common time basis, clearly a constraint to sound economic evaluation of alternatives. Similarly, the current section 7(a) of the Department of Transportation Act requires that agencies employ an admittedly inefficient standard to estimate the economic value of proposed waterway projects. This legal constraint not only constrains appropriate analysis, but almost certainly assures that projects will be undertaken which *decrease* rather than increase social welfare. When such constraints exist, it often takes legislative, executive, and judicial action to relax them. Until they are relaxed, their existence causes economic waste.

Administrative constraints—programs to be implemented require people to be hired, trained, and put to the task. For example, devising effective tax systems for less-developed countries may be unrealistic without the administrative process and personnel to administer them. Indeed, many believe this constraint is the primary limitation on good economic analysis in the federal government.

Distributional constraints—as we have seen, public expenditure and investment programs are often made to serve income distributional as well as economic efficiency goals. Such expenditures may be undertaken only if they demonstrate certain patterns of income generated by regions, income classes, and generations. If this pattern of income exists, the broad objective of "maximum income per capita" may be constrained in order to obtain a certain pattern of income distribution.

Political constraints— the process of decision making itself is costly, time consuming, and often frustrating. Indeed, optimal social solutions may not be realizable in the practical politics of the moment. As with the distributional contraint, some short-term real income or economic welfare may be sacrificed to preserve political consensus or the very process of orderly decision making.

Financial or budget constraints—resource scarcity typically gets translated into monetary and budget scarcity. When budgets are limited for governments, departments, and agencies, systematic analysis must look for less than optimal solutions. Benefits must be maximized within the fixed budget. In a wider sense, and especially for smaller, less self-reliant countries, financial constraints include not only domestic budget limits, but also limits on foreign exchange.

In attempting to understand government decision making and the rule of systematic analysis in it, the role of constraints is critical; to ignore constraints is to depart from the real world. On the other hand, to regard all solutions except one to be blocked by some constraint is to remove the problem from analysis. If the analyst and policy maker are to be successful, they must recognize and work within constraints which are immutable and attempt to relax those constraints which place unnecessary impediments in the way of a full consideration of alternatives.

V. EXTERNALITIES: SIDE EFFECTS AND SPILLOVERS

It is in the very nature of model building to include some things and to exclude others from formal analysis, that is, to abstract. Variables or phenomena are grouped into classes or categories because of certain common qualities. Certain other characteristics they may possess are assumed to make no difference for the purposes of the analysis. Likewise, a number of categories are enclosed within the system of inputs and outputs being considered. Other inputs and outputs are excluded from the system, and their exclusion is assumed to make no difference to the solution.

Because of this practice, a crucial test of any analysis rests on the answer to the following two questions.

1. Are variables within classes, which are included in the model, grouped together in such a way that the analysis is not distorted? Are the similarities within a class sufficiently great to swamp any differences which such variables may possess? For example, is it safe to lump together the money costs of inputs irrespective of their origin (say, money wages paid to otherwise employed skilled workers as compared to money wages for otherwise unemployed, unskilled workers who might be used or trained)?

2. Are variables placed outside of classes and outside of the model so extraneous as to be neutral or null in their effect on the outcome of the model? Are there any variables omitted from the model which may seriously alter its results?

For example, can one legitimately ignore in government projects such considerations as the rate of reinvestment by the beneficiaries of the projects, the rate of population increase by such beneficiaries, or the probable tastes and preferences of future generations?

The philosophic underpinnings of Western science are keyed to the kind of sorting-out and placing-into-appropriate-boxes process necessary to successful analysis. Indeed, both the natural and social sciences proceed in this manner in developing hypotheses about and predictions of real world behavior. In Aristotelian terms, a thing is only A or non-A. In computer language (based on binary systems), a thing is either 0 or 1. In the economist's model of the market-oriented, profit-maximizing business firm, a decision counts only as it raises or lowers the firm's profits. Only changes that have an impact on profits are seen as contributing to decisions. Thus, the incidental social gains or costs which the firm may create (but for which it isn't compensated or doesn't have to compensate) are not taken to be of relevance in the firm's decision-making process.

The variables which are relevant to the decision are called "internalities," as they are included within the model, that is, relevant to the decision. Other variables which are taken to be *not* relevant to the decision are called "externalities," or "spillovers," or "side effects."

Internalities concern themselves with quid pro quo's between parties; externalities concern themselves with third parties getting in the same transaction some *quo's* for which no *quid's* are paid. That is, in the Pigovian sense, A in rendering a paid service to B also serves (or disserves) C for which no payment is made. In government decision making such external effects, often better called spillovers or repercussion effects, may be important in arriving at optimal solutions. The initial decision as to which effects to internalize must be checked at the end of analysis so that any externalities that do make a difference can be internalized.

This is a difficult but necessary ingredient in any analysis. Even though everything may be related to everything else, analysis is premised on the view that some things are more important than other things. In the Aristotelian world of Western science some things are in, the other things are out. In the Miletan world view, the world is one category: things are not in boxes but in process. In the West, man A steps into river A; in the Miletan world, in the language of Heraclitus, "The same man cannot step into the same river twice," as both the man and the river are changing. To arrive at solutions one must simplify reality and assume the Aristotelian world, but to make certain that the solutions are correct one must not forget the Miletan world. The externalities may be important. For example, river valley development à la TVA may be a proper government program for an underdeveloped region in one place at one time, but not so in another place, say Helmand Valley in Afghanistan, at another time.

The following is an example of an impact usually treated outside the formal model in government decision making. A large concrete and steel dam, when operating, would flood an enormous number of river valley areas. In analyzing the world of such an installation, the formal model analyzes the value of the flood damage which will be averted, the power which will be produced, the water supply which will be created, and the recreation which will be enabled. The formal model also analyzes the value of the resources which it will take to build and operate the installation. However, other effects—usually excluded in such models—may also result from the installation. Because the river valley is flooded, landscape and scenic views may be irreparably destroyed. Society may wish to use this river valley for a park or scenic area in future years. To fail to consider this spillover value in making the decision about whether or not to undertake the proposed dam would be to ignore an externality crucial to a public policy decision.

What are some of these "external effects" to be considered, especially when one moves from the private sector (concerned with private profits and consumer satisfaction) to the public sector (concerned with social benefits and social costs)? The four kinds of external effects or spillovers to which the analyst should be sensitive may be outlined as follows: (1) production to production (2) production to consumption (3) consumption to consumption, and (4) consumption to production.

1. *Production-to-production spillovers:* uncompensated activities by one producer often affect the quantity or quality of the output of other producers. Examples of this kind of externality are fairly common. For example, when one mining establishment pumps water from its mine, the production of other mines may be affected. When electric generating plants use river water for cooling purposes and return it, heated, to the stream, the output of the downstream fishing industry may be seriously affected. When government production decisions cause the production process of other producers to be affected, the analyst must account for this kind of externality.

2. *Production-to-consumption spillovers:* activities by producers often affect the environment of consumers or the quality of goods they consume. The existence of air, noise, and water pollution often has a major impact on the enjoyment experienced by consumers. In this case, as in the first (1), the government's activity as a producer, or its impact on other private producers, may create this externality. Again, the value of this spillover should be included in the evaluation model used by the analyst and decision maker.

3. *Consumption-to-consumption spillovers:* activities by one consumer (or groups of consumers) often affect the welfare of other communities. One thinks immediately of loud radio noise in a public park on a quiet Sunday afternoon. The government, it should be noted, often performs consumer functions and is, consequently, as liable to produce these consumer-to-consumer spillovers as any other consumer. When a private citizen, in "consuming" a highway imposes delays on other highway users, a spillover of this type is occurring. Similarly, when

personnel on government business impose congestion delays on the highway, there may be a spillover created of the consumer-to-consumer variety.

4. *Consumption-to-production spillovers:* activities by one consumer often affect producers—for example, a hunter, searching for game, destroys crops. In this variety of externality and in (3), the source of the spillover is somebody (something) engaging in consumption activity. In evaluating alternative policy choices, therefore, the public decision maker should take note of these impacts both when the government is a consumer itself and when its action changes the behavior of private consumers.

Effects such as we have described, while they may be appropriately omitted from the formal analysis of alternatives, must be explicitly considered in the overall evaluation. They may, indeed, be the final and critical determinant of the choice. As is clear, the range of considerations to be discussed for their repercussion effect is wide and may include physical interdependence (e.g., upstream storage reservoirs affecting downstream projects), population effects, local or national unemployment, rates of saving and reinvestment in different sectors of the economy, large and discontinuous changes in inputs, outputs, and technology, social overhead costs, long-run investment strategies, the value of options being foreclosed, manpower needs and human capital effects, changing human attitudes, balance of payments considerations, use of shadow wage, interest, and foreign exchange rates, backward and forward linkage in capital projects, local market and price structures, the influence on state and local government budgets, and so on.

While good decision making requires that the analyst and decision maker be sensitive to the existence of externalities and implement his analysis so as to insure that spillovers which do exist get discovered, it is also essential that the difference between "real" externalities and "money" (or "pecuniary") externalities be understood. It is difficult to think of a decision which does not impose some adverse spillover effects on people. From the point of view of the entire society, however, some of these effects represent real social costs, while others mean that the loss inflicted on someone is simultaneously an equal gain to someone else. These latter, called "income transfers," are not real spillovers, but only monetary spillovers.

For example, when the government constructs a waterway, some traffic is shifted from railroads to the waterway. Because of the shift, railroads lose revenues and profits. The question is: Is this loss for the railroads an "externality" which should be considered a social cost in evaluating the waterway? Analysts generally answer *no* because the loss to the railroads is only a monetary spillover, an income transfer. The revenue lost by the railroad is gained by the barge line; the stockholders of the railroads have lost, while the stockholders of barge lines have gained and, on balance, the society as a whole shows no net loss or gain.

A sure way of distinguishing between spillovers which are real and those which are only monetary transfers is by answering the following questions: Is there any real output or production which is destroyed or not undertaken because of the decision? Are any resources or productive inputs destroyed or caused to lie idle because of the decision? Is there, on balance, any loss of consumption (defined broadly to include all increments to people's satisfaction) or investment because of the decision? If the answer is yes, the spillover is real and should be considered.

This distinction between real effects and monetary transfers is pertinent to the discussion as to whether or not "secondary benefits" ought to be included in systematic analysis. These secondary impacts occur, for example, when a beneficiary of the output of a public project spends some of his supplemental income, thus increasing the prices of certain products and the incomes of the producers of those products. The critical question is: "Is the increase in the income of this producer an increase in real national income or is it only an income transfer?"

Nearly all experts have found that the vast bulk of impacts referred to as "secondary benefits" are only income transfers and thus should not be counted in systematic analysis. However, other externalities which do affect real output must be counted.

VI. TIME: THE INTEREST RATE PROBLEM

Thus far we have simplified benefit-cost analysis by keeping it in a certain, timeless world. Objectives are ascertained and quantified, in dollars usually; constraints, including costs, are ascertained and quantified. Thus the achievement of our objectives becomes limited by scarcity and the list of feasible solutions shrinks; but if any feasible solutions remain, we do arrive at a definite solution to our type I—maximize benefits—or type II—minimize costs—problem. To arrive at this point and to reach a definite solution we have abstracted from reality only a partial selection of objectives and constraints, assuming that the internalities were the critical variables and that the externalities will not make any significant difference in our decision-making process.

But now time enters. We have already abstracted the bits and pieces of phenomena (benefits and costs) into dollar boxes. But in a world of time a dollar is not a dollar. A dollar has a specific value only on a specific date. (We assume money is in banks and not in the ground.) Thus, yesterday's dollar is equal to $1.05 today, at 5 percent interest per day, and $1.1025 tomorrow. Likewise, tomorrow's dollar is worth only 95¢ today. A dollar's value becomes a function of time.

Our previous analysis took the stuff of reality and put it into homogeneous boxes of benefit dollars and cost dollars so we could compare and decide. Now our homogeneity and means of comparison again disappear as dollars are no longer equal to dollars. We must not only get the stuff of reality into dollar boxes but dollar boxes of the same date. This forces another decision: which date? Present value (telescope all dated dollar values to the present date) or terminal value (turn the telescope around and convert all dated dollar values to dollar values at the end of some project or time horizon). Remember again, the ultimate criterion for selection among spending choices (investment projects) is to maximize $(B - C)$ at some date; that is, to achieve the highest amount of net benefits at either a present or future date. Use of an internal rate of return criterion achieves an optimum and thus can be equated to this other criterion only under certain conditions.[4]

Thus, the crux of decision making is comparison, and the crux of comparison is getting stuff into homogeneous boxes. Apples cannot objectively be compared to pears; it becomes a matter of subjective taste rather than objective science. But then to avoid dangers of green or overripe fruit, we must get fruit of the same date of ripeness. Then we can decide: two ripe fruits are better than one on the basis of our decision making criterion that more is better than less.

Timing Benefit Streams: Time Preference

Consumption now is preferred to consumption later; a bird in the hand is worth two in some certain future bush. But at what rate do we discount future birds? Or what length of time equates the bird in the hand with the two in the bush? Do we accept the rate of individuals' time preference expressed by market rates of interest, say 5 percent, as for risk-free, long-term government bonds? Do we use a lower "social" rate, say 3 percent, including considerations for unborn generations, or do we assume that short-sighted individuals should not judge for society because of their "defective telescopic faculty"? (Pigou) Do we accept a view of interdependence among individuals' choice making so that one's own preference is partly determined by other choices or by mutually determined or autocratically chosen rates of time preference? What we really have is not one rate but a schedule of rates depending on a host of factors: the amounts of present and future goodies involved (with or without assumptions as to diminishing marginal utility of income or goodies), the rate of growth of these goodies, and the expected life spans of individuals and societies to consume these goodies. The nature of the choice itself among rates has to be determined—by people voting with dollars in the market place or by ballots in the polling booth. Economists have no set answer except that rates determined by imperfect capital markets and reflecting private instead of social interests are not the only (or best) rates to use.

4. Where projects are not interdependent or mutually exclusive, where starting dates are given, where no constraints (budgets) are operative, where the reinvestment rate is the same as the internal rate of return, where benefit and cost streams do not fluctuate wildly over time. See Prest and Turvey, *Economic Journal*, December 1965; also J. Hirshleifer, "On the Theory of Optimal Investment Decision," *Journal of Political Economy*, August, 1958, pp. 329–352.

Timing Cost Streams: Opprotunity Cost of Capital

Costs for economists are measured in terms of opportunities foregone. Spending $100 million in the public sector means that there is $100 million less spent in the private sector on either investment or consumption goods, assuming fully employed resources. If resources are not fully employed, government spending merely reduces enforced leisure, i.e., unemployment. Thus, the opportunity cost of capital is really a set of schedules reflecting different rates of return from alternative uses of different amounts of capital. *If* the goal of benefits desired is rapidly growing gross national product (GNP), then the equalization principle would prevail. Thus, resources earning, say 15 percent in U.S. manufacturing, would be clearly misallocated if they were shifted to government investment projects producing a stream of benefits at an annual rate of only 4 percent. If the resources are garnered by tax dollars instead of bond dollars, then, following Eckstein, the incidence of the chosen tax among income groups might measure increased borrowing costs, reduced investment yields, reduced consumption values, and so on. The critical test hinges on exactly what opportunities are foregone. The issue is not totally resolved, but there appears to be a growing consensus for much higher interest rates (10–15 percent) in judging government investment projects.

Summing Up: A Guide to Action

1. For the decision maker the first operational issue is: what difference do interest rates make in any given decision? Thus, he can study how sensitive decisions are to differing interest rates, say 5–10–15 percent. Some economists have found that a range of 4–8 percent in interest rates makes little difference.

2. For social welfare projects (health, education, urban renewal, and so on) not justified by high interest rates (10–15 percent), the error is not in the use of a high interest rate but in the failure to include enough of the externalities or indirect benefits.

3. For certain public sector spending it may be more effective to convert the analysis to type II (cost-effectiveness: finding least-cost solutions) problems. Here it is assumed the benefits are chosen by public will or social values. Attempts to measure the benefits relative to a stream of future private consumption or GNP can be futile.

4. When there is a fixed budget over time, there is no opportunity cost of capital; however, a social discount rate should still be used to equate intertemporal lumps of benefits.

5. For state and local policy makers, or in any case involving suboptimization, the Machiavellian manager would be acting less than rationally if he did not use his borrowing costs, for instance tax-exempt municipal bond rates. He might well assume that, in this imperfect world of third bests, his low borrowing rate

reflects a national policy that prefers him to control greater resource allocation than would be possible at a higher "truer" discount rate. On the other hand national policy makers, such as those in the Office of Management and Budget or on the Joint Economic Committee of the U.S. Congress, want such suboptimizing resource allocators to get the right signals, i.e., discount rates.

6. Interest rates usually are important but there may be no one correct rate. The rate or rates to use depend on changing times, capital productivity, objectives, benefits and costs included and excluded in the analysis, and the level of optimization. Once more the answer rests on the initial determination as to how badly one wants consumption or investment, now or later, in the public or the private sector.

VII. RISK AND UNCERTAINTY

We so far have presumed that the world is risk free and certain. In so presuming, we neglected the fact that neither future benefits nor future costs are known with 100 percent certainty. Indeed, in many cases, the level of uncertainty is enormous—how can we measure accurately benefits that might not appear until the year 2000?

The fact, then, is that the streams of dollar benefits and costs projected by the analyst are not estimates of simple points in time. At best, they are probability distributions. Thus, the analyst knows something of the amount of risk involved in the estimate and can alter the values of these expected dollars by the chance of their actually occurring. At worst, the analyst doesn't know the probability distribution over time. He may only have some vague and subjective notion of some possible range of outcomes. In this case, he is faced with "uncertainty" and must deal with it as best he can.

In the case of sheer uncertainty, the analyst has three possibilities. First, if the streams of benefits and costs are irregular, he may allow for uncertainty by adjusting the annual levels of benefits and costs. In making these adjustments, he can try a "sensitivity analysis" to see how far wrong he can be in his expected values and still have the proper decision. He can set ranges of maximum and minimum values for his benefits and costs; he may know the limits of the ranges but not the probability distributions within them. The analyst can work with contingency allowances to offset the effect of some expected downward or upward bias in the analysis. He can change his objective from one of simple maximization to other strategies such as "maximin" or "minimax" or others which have been suggested. In the absence of any clear-cut response to uncertainty, any of these strategies are plausible. The important thing is that he makes known the level and "costs" of the uncertainty which is present.

Second, if the uncertainty or risk is a strictly compounding function of time, the analyst might simply alter the discount rate. However, this procedure should be used with caution because rarely is the pattern in which uncertainty increases with time similar to the pattern of compound interest. Note that, in this case, the discount rate should be increased when discounting benefits, but decreased in discounting future costs.

Third, if the risk or uncertainty is judged to be illusive after some time period, the analyst may wish to compare alternative programs or projects within a more limited time horizon. He may thus set terminal dates by which to standardize the analysis of different projects.

In all of these alternatives, it has been presumed that uncertainty is something undesirable—that people are willing to pay something to avoid it. All the approaches to uncertainty have argued, therefore, that uncertainty must be allowed for by decreasing the estimate of the present value of benefits or increasing the present value of the cost estimate. Some recent analysis, however, argues that uncertainty is not an "undesirable" for the public sector as a whole—that because a government undertakes such a large number of investments of so wide a variety of outputs, the uncertainty of benefits and costs present in any one investment can be removed from the decision process.

The treatment of the unknown future is thus a difficult and largely unresolved matter in benefit-cost analysis. While most observers agree that uncertainty needs to be hedged against, there is, in principle, no single, uniformly accepted method for adjusting benefit and cost estimates. In practice, this necessity to make allowance for the presence of risk and uncertainty is usually observed in the breach.

CONCLUSION

This survey of the theory of systematic analysis has provided only the conceptual framework—the set of boxes—with which the analyst will be concerned. These five boxes—objectives, constraints, externalities, time, and risk and uncertainty—are the places to sort out the stuff of reality. They affect all decisions. But the best decisions are those that embody good sorting rather than simply adding up the benefits and costs mechanically, once they are sorted.

Part Two: Case Studies

This part contains four case studies illustrating different types of analysis. In each instance, the "problem" is first presented, followed by an analysis of the problem.

The first case study describes a work-study program for educable mentally retarded (EMR) children, and outlines an evaluation study to determine how well the program is achieving its objectives.

The second case study deals with the problem of how best to provide swimming opportunities for residents of a Model Neighborhood in Dade County, Florida. After describing certain background information, including data on various possible alternatives, the case study presents the analysis performed by Dade County; then follows a brief critique of the analysis.

The third case study describes the problem of a shortage of classroom teachers for the early childhood handicapped. The state government involved has established four-year objectives in terms of providing service to a certain percentage of handicapped children. Preliminary analysis of this complex problem demonstrates the infeasibility of the initial objectives and the need for further analysis, taking into account realistic estimates of manpower availability.

The fourth case study deals with a classic cost-effectiveness problem: Should the Air Force F 10B (a fighter-interceptor) be equipped with bombs or missiles for ground-support operations? The statement of the problem is followed by an analysis of the problem and a series of comments on the analysis.

Evaluation of a Work-Study Program for Educable Mentally Retarded Children

In this case study,[1] the program is first briefly described in "The Problem." Then follows a brief synopsis of an evaluation to determine the degree to which the program is achieving its objectives.

THE PROBLEM

Several years ago, the city of Oakton launched a Work-Study Program for educable mentally retarded (EMR) children in the Oakton public school system.

The supervisor of special education for Oakton had observed that few EMR children were getting or holding jobs. Those who did get jobs began to "float" from one dissatisfied employer to another. Several teachers, who held the belief that these children needed assistance in finding jobs and holding them, went into the community to find employment for the children.

This type of teacher assistance was not considered very satisfactory. Accordingly, the supervisor of special education did an investigation and developed the following conclusions:

1. These children, slow to learn and adjust, needed to be carefully selected and they also needed postschool adjustment.
2. Jobs for these children were relatively few.
3. The number of educable mentally retarded children at the secondary level would be increasing in the years ahead.
4. The school and community would profit from properly placed and well-adjusted workers, and both would suffer from dissatisfied employers.
5. A joint effort between school and community must be made to plan for these children.

1. This case is based on a paper "The Work-Study Program in Ohio," by William Beitzel, published in *Work-Study for Slow Learners in Ohio,* Columbus, Ohio, 1965. It was prepared by Graeme M. Taylor, Management Analysis Center, Inc., of Washington, D.C., on behalf of the Bureau of Training, U.S. Civil Service Commission, and the Bureau of Education for the Handicapped, Office of Education, Department of Health, Education and Welfare (DHEW).

This case has been prepared for the purpose of class discussion; the views expressed in no way represent the views of the author, the commission, or DHEW.

The author wishes to express his gratitude to the officials of various state governments, the Bureau of Education for the Handicapped, and the Bureau of Training, all of whom gave so generously their time and interest. A special debt is owed to Frederick J. Weintraub of the Council for Exceptional Children for his cooperation and assistance.

6. Because of a limited number of school people capable of assisting these children to find and hold jobs, additional workers must be found to help with the problem.

7. To have several different teachers "scouting" the community for job opportunities was a duplication of effort.

As a result of these observations, it was decided to launch an organized program in cooperation with the Ohio Bureau of Vocational Rehabilitation. As a first step, a coordinator was hired.

The coordinator was employed by the Oakton Board of Education and was nominally responsible to the supervisor of special education. His primary responsibility was the development of a work-school program, as well as its interpretation and maintenance in the community. He sustained liaison among the schools, the State Department of Education (Division of Special Education and Bureau of Vocational Rehabilitation), and industry. His contacts with prospective employers had the purposes of determining the types of jobs available to slow learners; he then conferred with local high-school counselors in order to select pupils who had qualifications for jobs available. Placement was made by the coordinator. The supervision of pupils on jobs was the joint responsibility of the coordinator and the teacher-counselors.

The teacher-counselors were teachers in the slow learning program who knew the children well. They had helped to select the students finally placed in job situations and had done the many hours of counseling and job supervision that were necessary. They were given free time from teaching to do this.

The duties of the teacher-counselor relative to the work-school phase of the program were as follows:

1. Prepare and refer qualified students to the coordinator for job placement.
2. Counsel special education students in personal and academic matters.
3. Interpret the program to:
   a. the pupils involved
   b. the special education staff and total school faculty
   c. the balance of student body
   d. the parents of the pupils.
4. Maintain adequate records of:
   a. permanent cards
   b. case studies
   c. job evaluations.
5. Schedule programs:
   a. maintain adequate academic schedules, meeting the temporal needs of the work-training program, and the learning needs of the students.
6. Assist with on-the-job follow-ups and evaluations.

Originally, the program considered two plans of operation:

Plan I

1. Students classified as juniors—work half-day; attend school half-day.

2. Students classified as seniors—attend school six weeks; placed on jobs for six weeks.
3. In the senior year after successful school and job experience, the student should be graduated.

Plan II

1. Juniors work half-day; attend classes half-day.
2. Seniors on full-time jobs; attend class one night a week to help them with any skill which would better assure them of success on their jobs. This would also provide an opportunity for them to exchange ideas and work experiences.
3. Students would be graduated with their class in June after having a full year of successful employment and after having met the academic requirements.

In practice, both plans were used, including modifications of each.

In actual operation, the needs of participating employers dictated the length of co-op periods. Other determinants included the extent of part-time employment, the desirability of full-time work training prior to graduation, and the hours of employment. This program was considered to be consistent with the philosophy of realistic experience in the world of work. Consequently, the particular plan of each assignment was determined by the demands of the job, not by program edict.

Candidates eligible for participation in the on-the-job phase of the program were defined as all eleventh- and twelfth-grade students currently enrolled in bona fide special education classes for slow learners.

Trainees were those candidates selected and placed on the job. Determination of feasibility for assignment, to a large extent, was by trial and error. No consistent criteria for predetermined job success have been evolved. If a client, thus selected and subsequently placed, sustained job failure and was removed, he was returned to "candidacy" or "referral" status. Employer and client interviews, and a staff conference, attempted to determine what remedial measures (if any) might assist future successful work training assignment. To illustrate this point, intensive vocational evaluation and personal adjustment training were provided for some students by the Bureau of Vocational Rehabilitation through the facilities of a local private agency (Goodwill Industries). Remedial work was continued with those clients until successful vocational placement was sustained.

The majority of successful placements did not require such intensive services. Approximately half of the original training assignments became postgraduate placements. Those failing to adjust to their first placement were reassigned to another job as soon as it was feasible. The time between assignments in such cases depended upon the characteristics of the client and availability of training jobs.

Students assigned to work-training were placed on jobs in the community with cooperative employers who were aware of their limitations and capabilities. The jobs were always real. They were not created as "training" situations. Special concessions in work demands and wages were not allowed. Each did a "man's work" for a "man's pay."

ANALYSIS

Assuming the program described above has been operating in Oakton for a few years, design a program evaluation study to determine how well the program has achieved its objectives.

The purpose of any attempt at performing a program evaluation is to determine the degree to which the program has achieved its objectives. This requires a retrospective or historical audit of program accomplishments.

The following brief synopsis of one possible design of an evaluation of Oakton's work-study program for EMR children consists of four steps:
1. Clarification of the problem addressed by the program
2. Delineation of program objectives
3. Choice of measures of program output, effectiveness, and benefit
4. Design of the research plan

Various possible statements of "the problem" could be suggested; however, it is hard to improve on the simple statement: *Few EMR children are getting or holding jobs.*

Although deciding on a statement of the problem may be a simple matter, several statements of program objectives could be suggested, for example:
1. To improve employment opportunities for EMR children in Oakton
2. To permit EMR children in Oakton to lead meaningful lives where they can be economically self-sufficient
3. To locate job openings suitable for EMR children in Oakton and to train the children for these jobs
4. To train X percent of the EMR children in Oakton to secure jobs paying a minimum of $5,000 per year, and to hold them for at least one year

Each of the above statements, however, has certain defects. Statement (1) is much too vague. Statement (2) represents one way of phrasing the *ultimate* objective of the program, but is not particularly useful as the basis for an analytic program evaluation. Statement (3) describes the operation of the program, not its purpose. Statement (4) is, of course, much too specific.

The following statement avoids the above pitfalls, and will be adopted as our formulation of the objectives of the program:

To increase the percentage of EMR children in Oakton who are (*a*) placed in suitable jobs and (*b*) hold these jobs for a reasonable period of time.

It must be noted that the statement requires amplification. For example, what is meant by "suitable jobs," and how long is a "reasonable period of time"? But, these questions cannot be answered *a priori;* we must wait until some preliminary data have been gathered.

Before proceeding to choose appropriate measures of program output, effectiveness, and benefit, it is often useful to prepare a diagram or flow chart of the program under study. In the case of the EMR work-study program, a simplified flow chart might be drawn as indicated in Figure 1. A diagram of this sort is frequently helpful in systematically laying out the flow of events associated with the delivery of program objectives. It can help the evaluator focus his attention on key indicators of program success, and can be particularly useful in differentiating between intermediate and final outputs.

Figure 1
Flow Chart of Work-Study Program

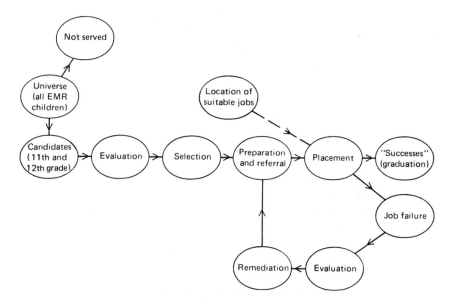

The following is suggested as a partial list of measures of program output, effectiveness, and benefit:

Output measures
1. Number of children enrolled in the training phase of the program by age, school, status of training, and type of training
2. Number of man-months of training provided
3. Number of referrals
4. Number of placements
5. Number of job failures (negative measure)
6. Number of "successes"
7. Number of jobs located
8. Number of cooperating employers

Effectiveness measures
1. Percent of all eligible children in Oakton who are actually enrolled in the program at various stages (a measure of the program's effectiveness in identifying and enrolling members of the target group)
2. Ratio of "successes" to enrollees; also, ratio of "successes" to total estimated population
3. Ratio of "job failures" to enrollees—one-time job failures, two-time job failures, etc. (a negative measure of effectiveness)
4. Percent who hold jobs for varying periods of time—e.g., one year, two years, etc.

(Clearly, the above measures of effectiveness become most useful when expressed in relation to the situation that would have existed *without* the program, i.e., measure of program *impact* on the problem.)

Benefit measures
1. Increase in expected lifetime earnings of graduate of the program.
2. Reduction in costs of maintaining members of the target group on public welfare.
3. Contributions by graduates to society—productive labor, taxes, support of themselves and their families, preserving families intact, etc.
4. Increase in feeling of self-esteem and personal satisfaction on the part of the graduates.

(Probably only items (1) and (2) are quantifiable to any useful degree.)

Clearly, data should be collected along the lines suggested by the various measures of output, effectiveness, and benefit listed above. In addition, *cost* and *control* data will be required. (The need for data on program costs is obvious and will not be discussed further.)

"Control data" consists of information of the following kinds:

1. data on the situation in *other comparable cities*
2. data (historical) describing the situation in Oakton *prior to the program*
3. data on children in Oakton who are *not covered* by the program.

Collection of data of the above kinds (collected according to the categories suggested above for measures of output, effectiveness, and benefit) will give the evaluator an indication of the incremental change brought about by the program in Oakton. After all, the evaluator is primarily interested in estimating the improvement in the number and percentages of children finding and holding jobs as a result of the program.

A most important point to be noted here is the desirability of building data collection procedures into the original design of the program. The program designer should anticipate the future need to continually monitor and evaluate the program, and should therefore design data collection procedures.

The description of the program given above suggests that extensive records are being kept on each child enrolled in the program. These records will probably constitute a major source of evaluative information. In addition, the program evaluator would probably need to (1) conduct a sample survey to estimate the total "universe of need" (2) interview employers to estimate qualitatively the performance of graduates (3) design follow-up data-gathering procedures to measure the length of time graduates remain in jobs, their earnings, reasons for quitting, etc.

Cost–Effectiveness Analysis of Swimming
Opportunities for Model Neighborhood Residents

In this case-study,[1] the problem is first described. Next, an analysis is presented. This analysis was performed by the jurisdiction involved. Finally, a brief critique of the analysis is given.

THE PROBLEM

In July 1968, a team of three analysts representing the Dade County (Florida) Park and Recreation Department, the Department of Housing and Urban Development, and the Dade County Community Relations Board were conducting an analytic study to determine the best method of providing swimming opportunities for residents of Dade County's Model Neighborhood. The decision to undertake this analysis had been made following a request by residents of Brownsville (a community within the Model Neighborhood) for construction of a swimming pool in Brownsville.

Data Gathered For the Study

Admission fees for pools operated by Dade County were 15 ¢ per day. The team had gathered the following information on the use of three county pools—see Table 1.

The population of the Model Neighborhood, as determined by a 1964 study, was 75,000; it was expected to be 80,000 by 1985. The area of the rectangularly shaped Model Neighborhood was nine square miles, consisting primarily of

1. This case was prepared by Graeme M. Taylor, Management Analysis Center, Inc., with the cooperation of Dade County, Florida, on behalf of the Ford Foundation and the State-Local Finances Project, George Washington University. This case is intended for class discussion only; while certain names and facts have been changed to avoid the disclosure of confidential information, this does not materially lessen the value of the case for educational purposes. This case is not intended to represent either effective or ineffective handling of an administrative situation, nor does it purport to be a statement of policy by the county involved.

The author wishes to acknowledge his debt to Gloria Grizzle, Budget and Analysis Division, Dade County, and J. Robert Perkins, Chief, Planning and Research, Park and Recreation Department, Dade County, for their cooperation and assistance in the preparation of this case.

34

single-family dwellings on small lots. The population was predominantly black; average family income was $3,000.

National recreational organizations had issued "rules of thumb" concerning the percentage of the population living near a pool that would use the pool on an average day; these estimates ranged from 1 to 5 percent. Various standards had been established for the minimum acceptable surface area of water per swimmer per day, ranging from 15 square feet to 30 square feet, with 19 square feet approximating Dade County's own experience. It was estimated that 1 1/2 miles was the maximum practical distance that any potential swimmer would walk to use a pool.

The analytic team had gathered cost information on two sizes of swimming pools, "standard" and "olympic." *Standard:* A standard pool has 5,000 square feet of water surface and requires a total of two acres of land. Construction costs were estimated at $127,900, including equipment. Operating expenses, including lifeguards' wages, were estimated at $20,800 per year. *Olympic:* An olympic pool is 11,700 square feet, and requires five acres of land. Construction and equipment costs were estimated at $278,900, and annual operating expenses at $39,100.

Land costs in the Model Neighborhood area were estimated at $120,000 per acre including acquisition, demolition, and relocation. Each acre of land, on the average, contained property returning $656 per year in property taxes to Dade County. The "life" of a pool was estimated to be 17 years.

It was possible to construct a pool at each of three locations in the Model Neighborhood area, selected such that all residents would be within a 1 1/2 mile radius of a pool. Several other sites were available. Six pools, for example, could be located so that all residents of the Model Neighborhood would be no more than 2/3 mile from a pool. County-operated swimming pools were normally open from March 15 to November 15.

Bus Swimmers to Crandon Park: Another possibility considered by the analytic team was to bus swimmers to Crandon Park, a Dade County beach park located approximately an hour's bus ride from the Model Neighborhood area. These busses would operate each day during the four summer months, and on 20 weekends during the remainder of the year, for a total of 162 days of operation. Crandon Park contains a zoo, various amusement rides, and other attractions such as miniature golf and skating. Busses and drivers could be hired for $44 per bus per day; each bus could carry 72 passengers. It was considered desirable to have one adult recreation leader for every 30 children; the leader's wages would be $18.25 per day. Admission to the beach and all amusement attractions was free. The beach was supervised by lifeguards employed by the county; it was anticipated that no additional lifeguards would be necessary if children were bussed from the Model Neighborhood. Public transportation operated between the Model Neighborhood area and Crandon Park; however, service was limited and several changes were necessary.

ANALYSIS

Goal and Objective

The Draft Program Structure states that the broad goal for the Leisure Time
Activities program area is to provide a wide variety of cultural and recreational
opportunities.

This paper will be concerned with one specific objective which falls within the
umbrella of this broad goal: to provide adequate opportunities for swimming
within the Model Neighborhood area.

It will be noted that only one pool is located in the Model Neighborhood. As
an example of the demand, between two and three hundred children daily attend
morning swimming classes at this pool during the summer.

Measures of Effectiveness

In order to evaluate the effectiveness of the alternatives to be considered, the specific objective should be stated in more concrete terms. To provide "adequate
opportunities," it will be necessary to estimate how many people would be expected to avail themselves of the opportunity at any one time and how much
water surface should be available for each swimmer.

There is no one standard universally accepted for the amount of water surface
which should be provided for each swimmer. Standards established by various
recreational associations range from 15 to 30 square feet per swimmer. Based
upon familiarity with facilities provided by the Dade County Park and Recreation Department, it was concluded that the suggested standard of 19 square feet
of water surface per swimmer was adequate.

Estimates of the percent of total population which would avail themselves of
swimming at any one time also varied. National recreational organizations gave
rules of thumb which ranged from 1 to 5 percent. Experience with neighborhood
swimming pools in Dade County indicates that the 5 percent estimate is too high.
The average attendance on a summer day for three of the pools is shown below:

Table 1
Pool Attendance

Neighborhood pool	Attendance	Population living within a 1 1/2 mile radius of pool	% of popu- lation using pool on a given day	Type of neighborhood
Bunche Park	150	18,000	0.8%	poor, black
Richmond Park	200	5,750	3.5	upper-middle black
Cutler Ridge	350	10,000	3.5	upper-middle white

The American Society of Planning Officials has taken the following position: "Public pools are generally designed to accommodate the maximum attendance at one time on an *average* day. As in many other municipal facilities, it is not economical to design for the days of maximum attendance, since the cost of maintaining a pool adequate for peak loads would be prohibitive. *Overcrowding on peak days is preferable to excessive space and high operating costs throughout the swimming season.*"

Based upon this information, it appeared that facilities which would accommodate 2 percent of the population at any one time would be adequate. It is estimated that in 1985 the population in this area will be 80,000. The 1964 population estimate for this area, made as a part of the Metropolitan Urban Area Transportation Study, was 75,000. Because the population will remain relatively stable, facilities adequate to fill the need for a population of 80,000, if provided within the next year or two, should remain sufficient for the next 15 to 20 years. This means that facilities which would serve 1,600 people at any one time (2% of 80,000) should be adequate to fill the need.

Criterion

The test of preferredness to be used in evaluating the alternatives will be to provide 19 square feet of water surface for 2 percent of the population at minimum cost. The objective will be held constant, and that alternative which will attain the objective at least cost is to be preferred.

While one alternative may best meet the criterion established, other alternatives may offer indirect benefits. These, as well as indirect costs, will be pointed out for each alternative.

Constraint

In order to assure that swimming opportunities would be accessible to the Model Neighborhood residents, a limit was placed on how far a person could be expected to walk to avail himself of the opportunity. It was assumed that the average person could walk a mile in 15 minutes. A maximum distance of 1 1/2 miles was set, which should not require more than half an hour's time.

Alternatives

In summary form, these are the three alternatives to be considered:
A. Construct six standard-size swimming pools in the Model Neighborhood area
B. Construct three olympic-size swimming pools in the Model Neighborhood area
C. Bus Model Neighborhood residents who want to swim to Crandon Park.
The cost data for each alternative is subject to relatively few uncertainties. The

cost of constructing pools is known (based upon the experience of the Park and Recreation Department) except for the cost of land acquisition, which was estimated by the Department of Housing and Urban Development. Rates for the use of busses are also known. The greatest uncertainty lies in the rate of increase in costs of construction, maintenance, and operation due to inflation. For purposes of this analysis, constant 1968 dollars have been assumed throughout.

Another cost problem lies in the difficulty of equating a dollar invested in the provision of swimming opportunities today with a dollar invested 15 years from now. The first two alternatives require major capital investments during the first year, while the third alternative requires a more even level of investment for each year that the program is carried out. It has been assumed that the swimming pools would be usable through 1985. In order to equate the three investments, the cost stream for each alternative has been discounted back to 1968, using a 7 percent discount rate. Total costs for each alternative have been shown both before and after applying the discount rate.

Table 2
Cost of Pools

	Total Net Cost (in thousands of dollars)				
	Construction	*Operating*			
Alternative	*1968*	*1969*	*1970*	*1971 · · · 1985*	*Total*
A	2,207	106.8	106.8	106.8 106.8	4,023
B	2,637	99.3	99.3	99.3 99.3	4,325
C	-0-	313.5	313.5	313.5 313.5	5,329

Table 3
Comparison of Discounted and Undiscounted Costs

Alternative	*Discounted at 7%*	*Undiscounted*
A	$3,250,000	$4,023,000
B	3,606,000	4,325,000
C	3,060,000	5,329,000

Costs and Benefits of Alternatives

The costs and benefits of each alternative will be outlined in some detail below.
They are summarized in Table 4.

A. Construct six 5,000-square-foot standard pools, each accommodating 263
    people at a given time.
    1. Land Costs $1,440,000
        a) Two acres required per pool, or twelve
            acres total
        b) $120,000 per acre includes acquisition, demo-
            lition, and relocation
    2. Construction Costs, $125,000/pool × 6 pools $ 750,000
    3. Equipment Costs, $2,900/pool × 6 pools   17,400
    4. Operating Costs
        a) Expenses $20,800/pool/year
        b) Income   - 3,000/pool/year
        c) Net $17,800/pool/year
                        _____ × 6 pools
                        $106,800/year
                        _____ × 17 years
                        $1,815,600 $1,815,600

                                        Total Cost $4,023,000

    5. Benefits of A
        a) Can be located within 2/3 mile (approx. 10 minute
            walk) of each resident
        b) Best opportunity for individual swimming
            instruction
        c) Can accommodate 1,578 swimmers at any given
            time, compared to a calculated need to accom-
            modate 1,600
        d) No vehicular transportation with its safety hazards
            involved
        e) Trend toward smaller pools. Following quoted
            from American Society of Planning Officials:

"Experience has shown that several moderate-size pools, properly constructed,
with adequate water treatment and strategically located, will serve the community better than a single, very large swimming pool. *The trend is definitely toward smaller pools which meet official regulations and specifications.*"

B. Construct three 11,700-square-foot olympic-size pools, each accommodating 615 people.

   1. Land Costs $1,800,000

      a) Five acres required per pool, or fifteen acres total

      b) $120,000 per acre includes acquisition, demolition, and relocation

   2. Construction Costs, $275,000/pool × 3 pools   825,000

   3. Equipment Costs, $3,900/pool × 3 pools   11,700

   4. Operating Costs

      a) Expenses $ 39,100/pool/year

      b) Income   − 6,000/pool/year

      c) Net $ 33,100/pool/year
                             × 3 pools

               $ 99,300/year
                    × 17 years

            $1,688,100 $1,688,100

                                         Total Cost $4,324,800

   5. Benefits of B
      a) Can be located within 1 1/2 miles (approximately 20-to-25 minute walk) of each resident.
      b) Individual swimming instruction opportunity less than alternative A, but greater than alternative C.
      c) Intangible benefit to those who prefer a large pool.
      d) Can accommodate 1,845 swimmers at any given time, compared to a calculated need to accommodate 1,600.
      d) Some vehicular transportation anticipated, but not nearly so much as transportation to a beach.

C. Construct no pools, but bus swimmers to Crandon Park
   1. Costs
      a) Transportation

      >   44/bus/day
      >   X 22 buses/day, each with a
      >   capacity of 72 children
      > $ 968/day
      >   X 162 operating days/year
      > $ 156,816/year
      >   X 17 years
      > $2,665,872

      b) Staff—One Recreation Leader per each 30
         children

      >   53 adult recreation leaders (1
      >   for each 30 children)
      > $ 18.25/leader/day
      > $ 967/day
      >   X 162 operating days/year
      > $ 156,654/year
      >   X 17
      > $2,663,118

      c) Intangible Cost—two hours/day/participant lost to
         transportation (not quantified)
      d) Higher exposure to traffic accidents (not quantified)
      e) Least opportunity for individual swimming in-
         struction (not quantified)

      >   Total Tangible Costs $5,328,990

   2. Benefits of C
      a) Since 22 buses/day would be needed, pick-up points
         could be scattered throughout the area, conceivably
         making these points within 1/2 mile (approximately
         8 minutes walk) of each resident.
      b) Can accommodate 1,584 swimmers at any given time,
         compared to a calculated need to accommodate 1,600.
      c) Accommodations are flexible, and can be adjusted for
         more or fewer swimmers as needed.
      d) Intangible benefit of swimming at the beach rather
         than a pool, with many existing attractions already
         available such as the zoo, picnicking, amusement rides,
         miniature golf, skating, etc.
      e) Flexibility in changing program in future years due to
         lack of sunk costs.

Table 4
Provision of Swimming Opportunities for Residents of the Model Neighborhood
A Comparison of Alternative Costs and Benefits

	Alternatives		
	A	*B*	*C*
Costs and Benefits	*6* *Standard Pools*	*3* *Large Pools*	*Bus to Crandon Park*
Costs Total Net Cost			
Not discounted	$4,023,000	$4,325,000	$5,329,000
Discounted	3,250,000	3,606,000	3,060,000
Sunk Cost[a]	$2,207,000	2,637,000	-0-
Benefits Opportunity for individual swim- ming instruction	Best	Intermediate	Least
Proximity of facility to resident	Closest	Intermediate	Farthest
Traffic hazards	Fewest	Intermediate	Most
Swimmers who can be accommodated at a given time[b]	1,578	1,845	1,584
Availability of other attractions		Intangible benefit for those who prefer large pools	Beach, zoo, picnick- ing, amusement rides, other recrea- tional facilities

a. The smaller the sunk cost, the greater the flexibility in expanding or reducing, or otherwise changing the program in future years.
b. Need was estimated at 1,600.

COMMENTS ON THE ANALYSIS

The above analysis was prepared by a three-man team in Dade County. The following nine comments are intended to draw the reader's attention to certain
features of the analysis, and to offer some suggestions for deepening and broad-
ening the analysis.

1. In general, the presentation of the above analysis is excellent and requires little comment. However, a few observations on particularly noteworthy features follow.

(*a*) The analysis is written in extremely clear, simple, straightforward language, with no attempts to "dress up" the report or to gloss over assumptions. This is a rare virtue.

(*b*) Table 4 represents a very interesting format for comparison of the alternatives, including nonquantifiable factors.

(*c*) The derivation of the effectiveness criterion is clearly and logically established at the outset of the analysis.

2. *Alternative discount rates:* The original analysis has been recalculated using 4 percent and 10 percent discount rates in Table 5. This indicates that the comparison *is sensitive* to the choice of discount rate.

Table 5
Revised Discount Rates

Alternative	Discounted Costs ($ million)			
	0%	4%	7%	10%
A	4.02	3.51	3.25	3.06
B	4.33	3.85	3.61	3.44
C	5.33	3.81	3.06	2.51

3. The original analysis did not take into account the opportunity cost of property taxes foregone on land used for swimming pools. This would modify the figures as follows:

Alternative A (six standard pools): 12 acres × $656 per acre per year = $7,872 per year in property tax revenues foregone. Undiscounted, this amounts to an additional $134,000 to be added to the total cost to Dade County of alternative A. At a discount rate of 7 percent, approximately $80,000 should be added to the cost of alternative A.

Alternative B (three olympic pools): 15 acres × $656 per acre per year = $9,840 per year in property tax revenues foregone. Undiscounted, this amounts to an additional $167,000 to be added to the cost of alternative B. At a discount rate of 7 percent, approximately $98,000 should be added to the cost of alternative B.

4. Apparently, no charge is involved in the alternative which busses children to Crandon Park, whereas 15¢ per child per day is contemplated for admission to the swimming pools. Perhaps the alternatives would be more truly comparable if revenue from this charge were excluded from the calculations. The effect is shown simply in Table 6.

Table 6
Revised Admission Charges

Total additional cost if admission charges are eliminated	Alternatives A or B
Undiscounted	$306,000
Discounted	$180,000

5. *Revised Comparison of Alternatives:* Incorporating the two modifications discussed in points (3) and (4) above, the comparison of the three alternatives presented in Table 2 of the original analysis is shown in Table 7.

Table 7
Revised Partial Comparison

Alternative	Total Costs	
	Discounted at 7%	Undiscounted
A	$3,510,000	$4,463,000
B	$3,884,000	$4,798,000
C	$3,060,000	$5,329,000

6. It should be noted that alternatives *A, B,* and *C* do not produce identical outputs; they differ in certain important respects.

For example, the olympic pool requires 5 acres of land, whereas the standard pool requires 2 acres of land. And yet the olympic pool itself has *less* than 2 1/2 times the capacity of the standard pool. The reason is, apparently, that the olympic pool envisioned in the analysis is not merely a larger version of the standard pool. The olympic pool would have seating capacity for spectators, and more parking spaces. Hence, it would be suitable for competitive swim meets or exhibitions. The olympic pool would also be two or three feet deeper at the deep end than the standard pool and would have a diving platform. The olympic pool, therefore, is more than simply a large neighborhood pool.

Both standard and olympic pools would be built within the model neighborhood—visible signs of improvement of the amenities. The Crandon Park alternative, however, would *not* improve the neighborhood itself, but it *would* expose neighborhood children to a variety of diversions at the beach.

Also, the alternatives differ in number of swimmer-days possible. Pools are open from March 15 to November 15, i.e., a total of 246 days per year.

Alternative A thus has a "capacity"[2] of (1,578 × 246) = 388,000 swimmer-days per year.

Alternative B has a "capacity" of (1,845 × 246) = 454,000 swimmer-days per year.

Busses to Crandon Park would operate on 162 days per year. Therefore, alternative C has a "capcity" of (1,584 × 162) = 257,000 swimmer-days per year.

Thus, we divide the *revised* discountec costs shown in (5) by 17 times the above "capacity" figures to get figures in Table 8. It must be noted, however, that the Table 8 figures are misleading in that the pools would probably *not* be used to capacity on every day between March 15 and November 15 each year. Assuming 75 percent, and then 50 percent, utilization of the pools over the entire period, we see differing results in Tables 9 and 10.

Table 8
Revised Swimmer-day Costs: Using Pools' Total Capacity

Alternative	Discounted Cost per Swimmer-day	Undiscounted
A	$.53 (i.e., divide $3.51 million by 17 × 388,000)	($ .68)
B	$.50	($ .62)
C	$.70	($1.22)

Table 9
Revised Swimmer-day Costs: Using 75% Pool Capacity

Alternative	Discounted Cost per Swimmer-day	Undiscounted
A	$ .67	($ .91)
B	$ .71	($ .83)
C	$ .70	($1.22)

Table 10
Revised Swimmer-day Costs: Using 50% Pool Capacity

Alternative	Discounted Cost per Swimmer-day	Undiscounted
A	$1.06	($1.36)
B	$1.00	($1.24)
C	$ .70	($1.22)

2. "Capacity" computed assuming 19 square feet of surface per swimmer.

7. *Other comments:* The following are some miscellaneous points.

(*a*) *Validity of the criteria:* The analysts should have, at least briefly, explored the implications of adopting different criteria than those used in their analysis. For example, perhaps the standard of 2 percent as the percentage of population to be served is not appropriate for the Model Neighborhood. One could argue either (1) that the Model Neighborhood residents may have more need of swimming opportunities in that their alternate means of recreation are more limited than residents of more affluent communities or (2) that the experience of the Bunche Park pool (0.8 percent of population using the pool—similar population composition) indicates that the 2 percent figure is too high!

Another standard used was 1 1/2 miles as the maximum distance any potential swimmer should have to walk to a pool. What would be the implications of altering this to, say, 1 mile or 2 miles?

A third standard was the figure of 19 square feet per swimmer per day. What would be the implications of altering this—say, by calculating pool needs at the extremities of the 15–30 square feet range suggested in the case?

(*b*) *Other alternatives:* Perhaps other alternatives might have been considered, for example a *combination* alternative involving, say, one or two pools with limited bussing; this would provide some variety for the users.

(*c*) *Reaction of Key Biscayne residents:* One factor which would almost certainly have to be considered would be the possible reactions of residents of the Crandon Park area to the bussing of Model Neighborhood residents.

(*d*) *Residual value of land:* One more modification might be considered. The three alternatives were compared on the basis of an expected 17-year "life" for the pools. A component of the investment cost was the acquisition cost of the land. Clearly, the land involved will have value to the county after 17 years— quite probably more than its original cost, even in 1968 dollars. After 17 years, the county could either sell the land, put it to an alternate use, or renovate the pools. We do not know the value of the land after 17 years; however, for purposes of illustration, let us assume that the value of the land is $100,000 per acre. The following crude adjustments could be made:

Alternative A (6 standard pools): 12 acres X $100,000 = $1.2 million

Alternative B (3 olympic pools): 15 acres X $100,000 = $1.5 million

Present value @ 7 percent discount rate:

A. $1.2 million X 0.320 = $0.384 million
B. $1.5 million X 0.320 = $0.480 million

Subtracting these figures from the revised figures shown in Table 7 gives us the new data in Table 11.

Table 11
Revised Land Costs

	Total Costs	
Alternative	Discounted at 7%	Undiscounted
A	$3,126,000	$3,263,000
B	$3,404,000	$3,298,000
C	$3,060,000	$5,329,000

8. *What additional information might be needed by the responsible Dade County official before reaching a final decision?* Clearly, officials in Dade County would have a perspective on the problem that is not presented in the case. They would be aware of information such as the following:

-magnitude of the Park and Recreation budget (to give perspective on the feasibility of committing several millions to swimming opportunities)

-other problems in the Model Neighborhood which may be more pressing than provision of swimming opportunities

There are, however, some items of information that would be helpful in reaching a final decision and which Dade County officials may not have readily at hand. For example:

-opinions of residents as to *their* preferences for large pools vs. small pools vs. bussing (perhaps a sample survey could be taken)

-to what degree would the various alternatives serve a hard core of "repeat" swimmers versus encouraging broad usage of pools?

-age and sex distribution of residents of the Model Neighborhood (which may have a bearing on the number and size of pools to be provided)

-implications countywide of abandoning the 15¢ admission charge for Model Neighborhood pools

9. *Summary:* Table 12 summarizes the quantitative results of the revised analysis. It is difficult to make a firm recommendation based on these results.

As is usually the case in analysis, the information presented does not enable the decision maker to make a clear-cut choice; multiple criteria exist and must be recognized. The job of the analyst, however, is to present the trade-offs involved.

The cost differences shown in Table 12 are not sufficiently great, given the many assumptions, to warrant a clear-cut choice of one alternative. It is likely that the decision will have to be made on the basis of "nonquantifiable" factors, some of which are discussed earlier in this note with others summarized in the original analysis in Table 4. It would be an instructive exercise for the reader to develop for himself a more complete display of nonquantifiable factors.

Table 12
Summary of Revised Calculations

Alternative	Revised total cost		Population served/day	Days available/year	"Capacity" in swimmer-days/year (000)	Revised cost per swimmer-day at various utilization rates discounted and (undiscounted)		
	Discounted at 7% ($ millions)	Undiscounted ($ millions)				100% ($)	75% ($)	50% ($)
A	3.510	4.463	1,578	246	388	.53(.68)	.67(.91)	1.06(1.36)
B	3.884	4.798	1,845	246	454	.50(.62)	.71(.83)	1.00(1.24)
C	3.060	5.329	1,584	162	257	.70(1.22)	.70(1.22)	.70(1.22)

Notes

1. The figures given for "population served/day" are based on dividing the area of the pools in square feet by the selected factor of 19 square feet per swimmer. For the bussing alternative, population served per day is based on 22 buses/day each with a capacity of 72 children. (The "target" population is 1,600—i.e., 2% of the estimated population of 80,000.)

2. The "capacity" of the bussing alternative C is not restricted in the same sense as that of the pools, since presumably buses could be added or withdrawn to meet demand. The "population served/day" and "capacity" figures shown above for alternative C are therefore not absolutely fixed.

Manpower Planning for Services to Early Handicapped Childhood

In this case study,[1] the problem is first described. There follows a partial analysis of the problem and suggestions for further analysis.

THE PROBLEM

A recent study by the Midlandia Division of Special Education and the Department of Health and Social Services demonstrated that the percentage of children, from birth to five years of age, presently receiving publicly supported special education services in the state of Midlandia was 0.5 percent; for ages six to eight, the percentage was 40 percent. In response both to these findings and to a proposed Early Childhood Special Education bill introduced in the state legialature, the Midlandia Division of Special Education has developed operating objectives concerning handicapped children from birth to eight years of age, and a pattern of services designed to implement these objectives. The objectives adopted were:

1. That the Division of Special Education increase the percentage of service to handicapped children aged 0–5 from the present level of less than 0.5 percent to 60 percent in four years.
2. That the Division of Special Education increase the percentage of service to handicapped children aged 6–8 from the present level of 40 percent to 60 percent in four years.

The new pattern of service proposed by the Division of Special Education to reach these objectives involved increased use of subprofessionals, teaching assistants, audio/visual equipment and other teaching devices. However, despite the anticipated utilization of these resources, the director of special education recognized that Midlandia would have an increasing need for classroom teachers of handicapped children during the next five years.

Peter Patterson, formerly a member of the state Planning Office, had recently

1. This case was prepared by Brendan Heneghan, Management Analysis Center, Inc., on behalf of the Bureau of Education for the Handicapped, Office of Education, Department of Health, Education and Welfare (DHEW). The analysis of the case problem was prepared by Graeme Taylor, Brendan Heneghan, and William Hartman, all of Management Analysis Center, Inc.

This case study has been prepared for the purpose of class discussion; the views expressed in no way represent the views of the authors or of DHEW. The data in the case were drawn from a number of states; "Midlandia" was created as a vehicle for teaching purposes only.

been hired as a planner by the Division of Special Education. He was asked by the director, David Davidson, to determine (1) the number of such classroom teachers Midlandia would require in order to achieve its early childhood objectives; and (2) the best way to attract the required number of teachers.

Peter Patterson knew that 725 classroom teachers were presently serving handicapped children aged 6-8 in the public schools, and that 17 teachers were serving those aged 3-5 under the auspices of the Division of Special Education. He also possessed information concerning the present population of children aged 0-8; Table 2 presents data on the numbers of handicapped children in Midlandia by age and type of handicap.

Mr. Patterson estimated that the birth rate would remain constant at 125,000 new babies born per year for the next four years and that the proportion of handicapped children would also remain constant (at 13 percent). He also knew that the newly proposed pattern of service required no classroom teachers for handicapped children aged 0-2, and a student-to-classroom-teacher ratio of 25:1 for handicapped children aged 3-8.

The division had agreed on a timetable—see Table 1—to reach the objective of serving 60 percent of the early-childhood handicapped in four years.

Table 1
Proposed Service Objectives
Division of Special Education

Year	Percent of handicapped aged 0–5 receiving services	Percent of handicapped aged 6–8 receiving services
Present	0.5	40
After 1 year	10.0	45
After 2 years	20.0	50
After 3 years	40.0	55
After 4 years	60.0	60

A number of alternative methods of increasing the number of classroom teachers had been proposed. Sam Underwood, Chairman of the Special Education Department at the University of Midlandia, had suggested that the division should make efforts to work more closely with the universities to increase the numbers of students trained in special education. Dr. Underwood had provided estimates of the present and anticipated costs to the state of the one additional year of university training necessary for the development of special education classroom teachers (Table 3). These cost figures were considered reliable, and were expected to remain valid during the next five years. Studies had shown that 50 percent of students presently graduating in special education from

Table 2
Handicapped Children in Midlandia (by age and type of handicap)[a]

	Total pop.	Total handi-capped	Mentally retarded	Emotionally disturbed	Learning disabilities	Deaf	Visually handi-capped	Speech impaired	Ortho-pedic	Multi-handi-capped
Percent-ages	100	13	3	2	3	0.3	0.2	3.4	1.0	0.1
Age					Number of Children					
1	125,000	16,250	3,750	2,500	3,750	375	250	4,250	1,250	125
2	120,000	15,600	3,600	2,400	3,600	360	240	4,080	1,200	120
3	113,000	14,690	3,390	2,260	3,390	339	226	3,840	1,130	113
4	114,000	14,820	3,420	2,280	3,420	342	228	3,880	1,140	114
5	107,000	13,910	3,210	2,140	3,210	321	214	3,640	1,070	107
6	105,000	13,650	3,150	2,100	3,150	315	210	3,570	1,050	105
7	104,000	13,520	3,120	2,080	3,120	312	208	3,540	1,040	104
8	102,000	13,260	3,060	2,040	3,060	306	204	3,470	1,020	102
Totals	890,000	115,700	26,700	17,800	26,700	2,670	1,780	30,270	8,900	890

Note

Total school-age population in Midlandia is 900,000 (ages 6–17).

a. Totals may not add because of rounding.

Table 3
Costs of Training Special Education Teachers in Midlandia

Institution	No. of students now enrolled in one-year special education degree program	Present number of faculty	Maximum student/faculty ratio	Present total costs to state (per yr.) $	State cost per student at maximum student/faculty ratio—with present no. of faculty (per year) $	State cost per each additional faculty member (per yr.) $	State costs (other than faculty) per additional student above present max. (per year) $	Maximum student enrollment without major expansion of facilities
Univ. of Midlandia (main campus)	140	20	10:1	700,000	4,000	15,000	3,000	300
Univ. of Midlandia (campus #2)	50	6	10:1	320,000	6,000	20,000	4,000	100
Teachers College	90	12	10:1	500,000	5,200	18,000	3,500	200
All other colleges	120	12	10:1	360,000	3,000	12,000	2,800	150

Midlandia's state universities take public school teaching positions within the state.

The Special Education Classroom Teachers Association had suggested that efforts be made to attract retired special education teachers back into the work force since the proposed new pattern of services made the position of classroom teacher more attractive to many. In fact, the association had recently conducted an opinion survey of retired special education teachers concerning the proposed new pattern, and found that most considered the change a major improvement despite Midlandia's continued relatively low salary scale. The study concluded that a promotional campaign costing $42,000 would attract 210 retired teachers back to the work force. Each retired teacher would require retraining costing an average of $800 before reentering the work force.

A third alternative considered by Mr. Patterson was a promotional campaign aimed at reducing attrition among special education classroom teachers. Based on experience in other states, Mr. Patterson estimated that a campaign costing $200,000 would reduce annual attrition from its present level of 15 to 12 percent; a campaign costing $500,000 would reduce attrition from 15 to 9 percent. (Attrition—teachers who leave the system during the school year—is expressed as a percentage of teachers employed at the beginning of the school year.)

Mr. Patterson estimated that Midlandia would probably continue to attract approximately 45 special education classroom teachers per year from out of state to teach in early childhood classes. Also, he assumed that, even without the promotional campaign suggested by the Special Education Teachers Association, approximately five retired special education classroom teachers each year would decide to resume teaching in early childhood classes in Midlandia.

ANALYSIS

This analysis is concerned with determining (a) the number of classroom teachers required over a four-year period in order to achieve certain service objectives, and (b) the most cost-effective combination of alternative methods to increase the supply of teachers adequately.

In summary, the analysis proceeds as follows: (1) The first step is to construct the base line—i.e., to compute how many teachers will be available without adoption of any new efforts. (2) The second step is to calculate the number of teachers who will be required each year if the division's newly proposed service objectives are to be met. (3) The third step is to consider the various alternatives presented in the case which would increase the supply of special education classroom teachers. The analysis demonstrates that, even if necessary funds are available, the alternatives given in the case would not increase the supply of special education classroom teachers to the level of need. Thus, either more realistic objectives must be established or additional alternative methods of attracting teachers must be discovered.

It should be emphasized that this analysis does not purport to be a rigorous analysis of the problem. Rather, it is intended to provide the reader with some of the basic calculations, and to offer some suggestions as to fruitful discussion topics.

Step 1: The "base line"

The first step in the analysis is to construct the "base line"—i.e., to compute how many teachers will be available without adoption of any new efforts.

We know that Midlandia presently has 725 special education classroom teachers serving children aged 6-8, and 17 teachers serving those aged 3-5. The total number of teachers at the beginning of the first year under consideration is therefore 742. Table 4 shows how the numbers of teachers at the beginning of each subsequent year are calculated. These calculations are based on several statements in the case:

1. Attrition will continue at 15 percent (i.e. 15 percent of teachers on board at the beginning of each year will leave the system—presumably through marriage, retirement, death, or leaving the state).
2. Each year, 45 out-of-state teachers will take positions in Midlandia teaching handicapped children (age 3-8).
3. Each year, 5 retired Midlandia teachers will resume teaching early childhood classes.
4. Each year, a certain number of new graduates of Midlandia's universities will take teaching positions in the state serving our 3-8 age group. This number is calculated as follows: Table 3 tells us that 400 students are presently enrolled in special education programs in the state's universities. If we assume that this represents a "steady-state" situation, then we can predict that 400 teachers will graduate each year.

The case tells us that 50 percent of students presently graduating in special education from the universities in Midlandia will take public school teaching positions within the state. Thus, 200 newly graduated special education teachers will join the system each year. However, not every new teacher will teach our target group—children aged 3-8. We must assume that the number of newly graduated teachers teaching the 3-8 group will be proportional to the percentage of the 3-8 age group in the total school-age population.[2] However, since there are now only 17 teachers serving those aged 3-5, compared with 725 teachers serving the 6-8-year-olds, it would probably be more reasonable to use the percentage of 6-8-

---

2. It is simpler to use total age-group figures for these calculations rather than numbers of handicapped children. We assume that the percentage of handicapped children remains constant at 13 percent; we also assume that 40 percent of handicapped children in the 6-8 age group will continue to be served. Since these percentages remain constant, we can therefore use simple population figures in lieu of number of handicapped children served.

year-olds in the school-age population. Table 2 in the case indicates that there are now 311,000 children aged 6–8 in Midlandia, compared to 900,000 school-aged children (i.e. aged 6–17). Now, 311,000 is 34.6 percent of 900,000. There-fore, we can assume that roughly one-third of the 200 newly graduated teachers will be serving our target group—67 teachers per year.

This figure of 67 teachers per year clearly applies to the first year. However, if Midlandia decides to expand its services to the handicapped aged 3–5, and launches programs to provide services to this age group, then we might expect that a certain number of graduating teachers will, each year, elect to teach this age group. Therefore, allowing one year to elapse before the newly graduating teachers can begin to serve the 3–5 age group, we can expect that newly graduating teachers will seek positions in proportion to the ratio of the 3–8 age group to the total 3–17 population. This ratio, from Table 2, is approximately 50 percent. Thus, after the end of the first year, we can expect to obtain 100 newly graduated teachers each year from Midlandia's universities.

Table 4

Calculation of "Base Line" Number of Teachers After 4 Years

Year	No. of teachers on board at begin-ning of year	Less: Attrition (15%)		Plus: out of state recruits (45 per yr)	Plus: retired teachers who re-sume teaching (5 per year)	Plus: new graduates (67 in 1st yr, then 100 per year)
		Attrition	Remainder			
1	742	111	631	676	681	748
2	748	112	636	681	686	786
3	786	118	668	713	718	818
4	818	122	696	741	746	846

Step 2: Number of Teachers Required to Meet Service Objectives

Table 5 shows the number of teachers required if the service objectives (Table 1) are to be achieved.

Table 5
Number of Special Education Classroom Teachers Required to Meet the
Division's Proposed Service Objectives

A. Ages 3-5

Year	No. of children in age-group	No. of handi- capped	Service target %	Service target number	No. of teachers required[a]
Present	334,000	43,500	0.5	380	17
After 1 yr.	347,000	45,100	10.0	4,510	180
After 2 yrs.	358,000	46,500	20.0	9,300	370
After 3 yrs.	370,000	48,100	40.0	19,240	770
After 4 yrs.	375,000	48,800	60.0	29,280	1,170

B. Ages 6-8

Present	311,000	40,500	40.0	16,200	725
After 1 yr	316,000	41,000	45.0	18,500	740
After 2 yrs	326,000	42,500	50.0	21,250	850
After 3 yrs	334,000	43,500	55.0	24,000	960
After 4 yrs	347,000	45,200	60.0	27,000	1,080

a. Using a student/teacher ratio of 25:1.

Recapitulating the base-line figures (Table 4) and the requirements figures from
Table 5 we can then construct Table 6 to illustrate the "teacher gap" that must
be filled in order to meet the division's newly proposed service objectives:

Table 6
"Teacher Gap" To Be Filled To Meet Service Objectives

Year	Base line no. of teachers	Teachers required to meet service objectives			"Teacher gap"
		Ages 3-5	Ages 6-8	Ages 3-8	
Present	742	-	-	-	-
After 1 yr.	748	180	740	920	172
After 2 yrs.	786	370	850	1,220	434
After 3 yrs.	818	770	960	1,730	912
After 4 yrs.	846	1,170	1,080	2,250	1,404

Step 3: Consideration of alternative methods of increasing the supply of teachers

The third step in the analysis is to consider the various alternatives, presented in the case, which would increase the supply of special education classroom teachers. The three alternatives identified are:

1. increase the number of special education students enrolled in Midlandia's universities
2. promotional campaign to attract retired teachers back into the work force
3. promotional campaign to reduce attrition.

Each of these alternatives is considered separately below:

1. *Increased enrollment at the universities:* This alternative is analyzed in Tables 7, 8, and 9. For the four institutions identified in Table 3, the marginal costs of adding additional graduates *without* adding faculty are shown in Table 7.

Column (1) of Table 7 shows the present annual costs (from Table 3). Column (2) gives the number of students presently enrolled (from Table 3). Dividing the present annual costs by the present enrollment figures, we obtain the figures in column (3), present average costs per graduate. The figures in column (4), maximum possible enrollment with present faculty, are obtained from Table 3 by multiplying the maximum student/faculty ratios by the present number of faculty. Subtracting the figures in column (2) from those in column (4), we obtain the figures in column (5), maximum number of additional graduates possible without adding faculty. Column (6) reproduces the figures from Table 3 giving the annual costs per student at maximum student/faculty ratio without adding faculty. These are multiplied by the maximum number of students, from column (4), to give the figures in column (7)—total annual costs at maximum student/faculty ratio, without adding faculty. Column (1) is then subtracted from column (7) to give column (8)—net additional costs of achieving the maximum student/faculty ratio. Finally, column (8) is divided by column (5) to give column (9)—cost per additional graduate.

In a similar fashion, Table 8 presents the method of calculation to derive the marginal cost of obtaining additional graduates by increasing the number of faculty to the maximum extent without a major expansion of facilities.

These results are summarized in Table 9 which ranks the various alternatives in ascending order of marginal cost per additional graduate. It can be seen, for example, that the cheapest alternative for the state would be to obtain additional graduates by simply increasing enrollment on the main campus, while the most costly alternative would be to expand the number of faculty on campus #2.

If all options were exploited to the maximum, a total of 350 additional graduates could be obtained each year at an additional annual cost of $1.5 million; the average cost per additional graduate would therefore be approximately $4,300.

Table 7
Marginal Annual Costs of Additional Special Education Students at Midlandia's Universities

	(1)	(2)	(3)	(4)	(5)	(6)	(7)	(8)	(9)
Institution	*Present annual costs*	*Present number enrolled*	*Present average cost per graduate*	*Maximum possible enrollment with present number of faculty*	*Maximum number of additional graduates possible without adding faculty*	*Annual costs per student at maximum student/ faculty ratio*	*Total annual costs at maximum student/ faculty ratio*	*Net additional costs of achieving maximum student/ faculty ratio*	*Cost per additional graduate*
	$		$			$	$	$	$
Univ. of Midlandia (main campus)	700,000	140	5,000	200	60	4,000	800,000	100,000	1,666
Campus #2	320,000	50	6,400	60	10	6,000	360,000	40,000	4,000
Teachers College	500,000	900	5,555	120	30	5,200	624,000	124,000	4,133
All other colleges	360,000	120	3,000	120	0	3,000	360,000	0	0

Table 8
Marginal Annual Costs of Additional Special Education Students at Midlandia's Universities—If More Faculty Are Recruited

	(1)	(2)	(3)	(4)	(5)	(6)	(7)	(8)
Institution	Maximum student enrollment without major expansion of facilities	Present maximum enrollment at maximum student/faculty ratios	No. of additional students possible (1) – (2)	No. of additional faculty possible (at 10:1 ratio)	Cost of adding maximum faculty	Non-faculty costs	Total additional costs required (5) + (6)	Cost per additional student
					$	$	$	$
Univ. of Midlandia (main campus)	300	200	100	10	150,000	300,000	450,000	4,500
Campus #2	100	60	40	4	80,000	160,000	240,000	6,000
Teachers College	200	120	80	8	144,000	280,000	424,000	5,300
All Other Colleges	150	120	30	3	36,000	84,000	120,000	4,000

Table 9
Summary of Results of Marginal Analysis
Sources of Additional Teachers Ranked in Ascending Order of Cost

		(1)	(2)	(3)	(4)
Institution	*Method*	*Maximum possible no. of additional graduates per year*	*Marginal cost per graduate*	*Total annual costs (2)×(3)*
			$	$
Main campus	Increase enroll-ment to maximum possible without adding faculty	60	1,666	100,000
Campus #2	Increase enroll-ment to maximum possible without adding faculty	10	4,000	40,000
All Other	Add faculty to maximum possible	30	4,000	120,000
Teachers College	Increase enroll-ment to maximum possible without adding faculty	30	4,133	124,000
Main campus	Add faculty to maximum possible	100	4,500	450,000
Teachers College	Add faculty to maximum possible	80	5,300	424,000
Campus #2	Add faculty to maximum possible	40	6,000	240,000
Total		350		$1,498,000

2. *Promotional campaign to attract retired teachers back into the work force:*
The case tells us that a campaign costing $42,000 would attract an estimated 210
teachers back into the work force, and that each teacher would require retraining
costing $800.

Table 10

Effects of Reducing Attrition From 15% to 9% in Combination With (1) Maximum Increase in Output of University Graduates, and (2) Maximum Number of Retired Teachers Persuaded to Rejoin the Workforce

| Year | No. of teachers on board at beginning of yr. | Less: Attrition (9%) | | Out-of-state recruits | Retired teachers | Add: "Normal" no. of new graduates | Max. no. of additional graduates | No. of teachers on board at end of year |
		Attrition	Remainder					
1	742	67	675	45	215	67	58	1,060
2	1,060	95	965	45	5	100	88	1,203
3	1,203	108	1,095	45	5	100	88	1,333
4	1,333	120	1,213	45	5	100	88	1,451

Therefore, this alternative could produce a maximum of 210 teachers at a total cost of:

$$\$42,000 + (210 \times \$800) = \$210,000$$

Thus, the average cost would be $1,000 per additional teacher.

3. *Promotional campaign to reduce attrition:* Determining the cost of this alternative, and its effect on the supply of classroom teachers, requires more complex calculations than the previous two alternatives. Because attrition is expressed as a percentage of the number of classroom teachers on board at the beginning of the year, the net effect of a reduction in the attrition rate in terms of the actual number of teachers "saved" each year will vary depending on whether or not this alternative is initiated in combination with, or in the absence of, either or both of the previous two alternatives.

Table 10 shows the calculations necessary to derive the number of teachers who will be available each year if (1) attrition is reduced from 15 to 9 percent (the maximum reduction mentioned in the case), and (2) all possible additional retired teachers (210) and new graduates (58 in the first year, and 88 thereafter) are obtained.

Table 11 compares the number of teachers *required* to meet the new service objectives (from Table 6) with the maximum number of teachers *available* (from Table 10). It can be seen that:

1. after 1 year, there is a surplus of 140 teachers
2. after 2 years, there is a small deficit of 17 teachers
3. after 3 years, there is a deficit of 397 teachers, which rises to almost 800 by the end of the fourth year.

Table 11
"Teacher-Gap" When All 3 Alternatives Are Employed

Year	Number of teachers required to meet service objectives	No. of teachers available	Surplus or (deficit)
Present	742	-	-
After 1 year	920	1,060	140
After 2 years	1,220	1,203	(17)
After 3 years	1,730	1,333	(397)
After 4 years	2,250	1,451	(799)

Thus, even if Midlandia were to employ all three alternatives, there would still be a shortage of teachers in the third and fourth years of the plan.

Reformulation of the Analysis

The next step is to reformulate the analysis. The reader might wish at this point to consider the question: What alternatives should now be explored? The options facing the Division of Special Education at this juncture might include the following:

1. Find new alternatives to increase the supply of teachers. These might include the following possibilities:

   (*a*) A more intensive campaign to attract retired teachers than the one contemplated in the case.

   (*b*) More intensive efforts to reduce attrition below 9 percent.

   (*c*) Increase the supply of newly graduated teachers from the universities by increasing the capacity of the universities (this would probably involve a major expansion of facilities), or by attempting to reduce the percentage of graduates who leave the state.

   (*d*) Attract more teachers from out-of-state.

   (*e*) Raise teacher salaries.

2. Revise the pattern of services for the early childhood handicapped. (For example, the student/teacher ratio could be increased.)

3. Revise the service objectives. (For example, the percentage of children to be served within four years could be reduced and/or the target date for achieving 60 percent service could be postponed.)

Brief comments on each of these possibilities follow.

Retired teachers: The case tells us that a campaign costing $42,000 would attract 210 retired teachers back into the work force. We cannot estimate from the information the potential pool of retired teachers as a source of additional teachers. It may be that a modest increase in our promotional efforts could attract another 100 retired teachers or it may be that 210 is the maximum feasible number without inordinate expenditures. We do not know the shape of the curve.

Figure 1
Possibilities for Attracting Retired Teachers

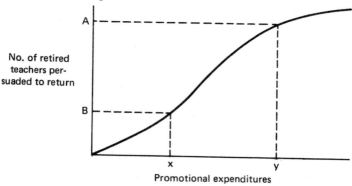

It may be that $42,000 is at point x in Figure 1 and 210 is given by point A. If this is the case, then the retired teacher pool would represent an attractive potential source of additional teachers. If, on the other hand, $42,000 is at point y and 210 at point B, then we have already reached the point of diminishing returns, and there would be no advantage in attempting to recruit additional retired teachers.

The major point to be made here is that Midlandia should try to estimate (1) the shape of the above curve, and (2) where the proposed $42,000 campaign lies on the curve, before pursuing this alternative any further.

Further reductions in attrition: Intuitively, it would appear that this alternative is not practical. An attrition rate of 9 percent is already very low.

Increased supply from the universities: A major expansion of the universities' capabilities would, in the long run, probably be the most desirable course of action provided Midlandia could reasonably expect to keep its "share" of the graduates. However, this alternative is costly and would require a long "lead time." It does not, therefore, hold much promise for solving our short-run problem.

On the other hand, it appears that efforts to increase the percentage of graduates who remain in Midlandia might be worthwhile. Presently, only 50 percent of newly graduated teachers remain in the state. Before attempting to design strategies to increase this percentage, the reasons for graduates leaving the state should be studied: Higher salaries elsewhere? Marriage? Returning to their home states? More attractive living or working conditions? Of course, one significant possibility might be that, until the present time, there was simply no demand for additional teachers in Midlandia, and graduates were forced to leave the state in order to find jobs. It may well be that, if additional teaching positions were created in Midlandia, more graduates would willingly remain in the state.

If the percentage of graduates remaining in the state could be increased from 50 to 75 percent, even assuming a 9% attrition rate, a considerable number of teachers could be added—see Table 12.

Table 12
Effects of Increasing the Percentage of Graduates
Remaining in the State From 50% to 75%

Year	Number of teachers on board at the beginning of the year	Less: Attrition (9%)		Add: Additional Graduates	Additional number of teachers on board at end of year
		Attrition	Remainder		
1	-	-	-	33	33
2	33	3	30	50	80
3	80	7	73	50	123
4	123	12	111	50	161

In Table 12, the figures for "additional graduates" are based on the following: as before, we assume 400 graduates per year. Of this number, 75 percent remain in the state; 75% × 400 = 300. In the first year, as before, we assume that 33 percent will be available for the 3-8 age group, or 100 teachers (instead of 67); in subsequent years, we assume that 50 percent will be available for the 3-8 age group, or 150 teachers (instead of 100). The increase in the first year is therefore 33 teachers, and in subsequent years the increase is 50 teachers per year.

This alternative would be even more attractive if we also increase the basic supply of new graduates (Table 9) by 350 teachers per year, as shown in Table 13.

Table 13

Effects of Increasing the Basic Supply of Graduates by 350 Teachers Per Year and Increasing the Percentage Who Remain in the State From 50% to 75%

Year	Number of teachers on board at the beginning of the year	Less: Attrition (9%)		Add: Additional graduates		Additional teachers on board at end of year
		Attrition	Remainder	From Table 12	By increasing the basic supply	
1	-	-	-	33	29	62
2	62	6	56	50	43	149
3	149	13	136	50	43	229
4	229	21	208	50	43	301

Thus, it is clear that this alternative would help considerably in reducing the "teacher gap." Table 14 illustrates this effect.

Table 14

Effect on Teacher Supply of Increasing the Percentage of Graduates Who Remain in the State From 50% to 75%

Year	No. of teachers on board at end of year (from Table 10)	Add: additional teachers at end of year (from Table 13)	Revised no. of teachers on board at end of year	"Need" (from Table 6)	Revised surplus (deficit)
1	1,060	62	1,122	920	202
2	1,203	149	1,352	1,220	132
3	1,333	229	1,562	1,730	(168)
4	1,451	301	1,752	2,250	(498)

Out-of-state teachers: The case does not contain any information on the potential of recruiting additional classroom teachers from outside Midlandia. It would seem, however, that the present figure of 45 teachers per year is rather low. Perhaps a study could be undertaken of the potential costs of an out-of-state recruiting campaign, and the estimated additional teachers who might be recruited each year.

Increased salaries: Before advocating this alternative, the Division of Special Education would certainly wish to conduct a careful study; this might include gathering such data as: (a) how many teachers leave the state to seek higher salaries? (b) how many retired teachers, or out-of-state teachers, could be attracted if salaries in Midlandia were higher? (c) where exactly does Midlandia stand in relation to other states in terms of salaries and working conditions?

Revise pattern of services: The proposed pattern of services should be studied to insure that the number of additional classroom teachers required has been kept to the minimum consistent with sound professional judgment.

Four years from now, there will be 722,000 children aged 3–8 in Midlandia (from Table 2). Of these, 13 percent will be handicapped—approximately 94,000 children. The presently proposed service objective calls for 60 percent to be served in four years, or 56,400 children. Thus, as shown in Table 5, an estimated 2,250 classroom teachers would be required. If, however, it were possible for one classroom teacher to serve *thirty* children (e.g. through even more intensive use of media, paraprofessionals, etc.) then the number of classroom teachers required would become 1,880—a decrease of 370 teachers.

Since the case does not give us details of the proposed pattern of services, we have no way of evaluating the feasibility of increasing the average student/teacher ratio. All we can recommend is that Midlandia should reexamine the proposed pattern of service in light of resource constraints (teacher shortage).

Revise service objectives: The presently proposed objectives call for 60 percent of handicapped children aged 3–8 to be served in four years. Suppose the achievement of this target were deferred one year? For example, let us assume that 50 percent are to be served in four years, rising to 60 percent in the fifth year. Then, in the fourth year, 47,000 children would be served instead of 56,400—a reduction of 9,400 children. Assuming the pattern of services is not changed and, therefore, the student/teacher ratio remains at 25:1, this would mean that 376 fewer teachers would be required at that time.

Conclusion

There are still many remaining avenues that could be usefully explored. The following suggestions are some of the possibilities:

- Elaborate on the opportunities to apply *marginal analysis.*
- Apply *sensitivity analysis* to identify the most critical assumptions.

- Explore the question of what are the truly *relevant costs* of each alternative. (Thus far, we have used costs to the state as a whole as the relevant cost measure. Should, perhaps, costs be considered from the viewpoint of the Division of Special Education? Or should private costs and opportunity costs be included, and the cost analysis be performed from a societal viewpoint?)
- Discuss the implications of various *qualitative factors* which have, thus far, been ignored.
- Perform new calculations starting with the resource constraint (i.e., an agreed-upon estimate of the maximum feasible number of teachers available each year) and *derive the service objectives* in light of this constraint.

Cost Effectiveness Analysis of
Bombs versus Missiles for the Air Force F 10B

In this case study,[1] the problem is first described. Then follows an analysis of the problem, and a series of comments on the analysis.

THE PROBLEM

In 1957 the U.S. Air Force initiated research and development work on a new fighter-interceptor, the F 10B. Design and engineering proceeded as scheduled, and in early 1961 prototype modes of the aircraft became available for evaluation and testing. On the basis of these tests the Air Force placed an order for 360 F 10Bs—a quantity sufficient to equip 15 air defense squadrons. Delivery was to begin in early 1962, with production scheduled at a rate of 18 aircraft per month.

During the period in which the Air Force was conducting tests of the F 10B the Secretary of Defense and Joint Chiefs of Staff (JCS) completed a thorough review of U.S. strategic policies and force structures. U.S. capabilities for limited war operations were given particular attention, and the review concluded that our forces were inadequate, especially for operations in remote geographic areas. The major deficiencies, in the opinion of the Joint Chiefs, were a lack of air transport capability, combat ready army forces, tactical ground support aviation, and sufficient stocks of conventional ordnance and ammunition. The Joint Chiefs suggested that the Secretary of Defense have the service departments review the JCS recommendations and submit proposals as appropriate. The Chiefs also proposed that the Joint Staff examine the desirability of establishing an additional specified command. The new command would be organized to conduct limited war operations on a worldwide basis. Operational control of units from all services would be vested in a single commander, who in turn would be subject to the direct control of the Joint Chiefs of Staff and the Secretary of Defense.

The Secretary of Defense accepted these recommendations. Subsequently, the service departments were directed to examine the Joint Chiefs' report and to develop recommendations for modification of the approved force structure.

1. This case study was prepared by Lt. Col. William P. Snyder, USA; it first appeared in *Case Studies in Military Systems Analysis,* published by the Industrial College of the Armed Forces, Washington, D.C., 1967. It is used here by permission of ICAF.

This material is furnished for instructional purposes only. The views or opinions expressed or implied are not to be construed as representing the official policies of the Department of Defense.

The Secretary's directive generated considerable interest among members of the Air Staff. The JCS report reiterated an argument advanced many times within the Air Force itself—that additional fighter-bomber aircraft were needed to provide an improved ground support capability. But which aircraft? The fighter-bomber aircraft then in service in Tactical Air Command squadrons was considered inadequate in many respects. The range and ordnance load of these aircraft were relatively limited; their inability to operate at any but very high speeds (500-550 kph) contributed further to their ineffectiveness in ground support operations. Nor, since the JCS report envisaged a rapid improvement in limited war capabilities, was there sufficient time to permit development of a new aircraft. For these reasons the Air Staff decided to examine several of the fighter-interceptors then in service with the Air Defense Command to determine which, if any, were suitable for ground support operations and what the time and cost of procurement would be.

One of the aircraft evaluated was the F 10B—and it proved surprisingly versatile in ground support operations. The Air Force therefore decided to request funds for eight additional F 10B squadrons (192 aircraft). Production rates were to be increased so that those aircraft would be available to Tactical Air Command by mid-1963.

The Air Force proposal to procure eight additional F 10B squadrons was circulated to other agencies and departments. The request was favorably received, except that the Army and Marine Corps requested additional information on the proposed ordnance load and fire control equipment of the F 10B. The Air Force noted that the F 10B would be equipped with two 20-mm machine gun pods, and would in addition be able to carry eight 4″ rockets and either ten 500-pound bombs or six napalm containers. "The F 10B," the Air Force statement continued, "can be modified easily and quickly to carry these items. Tests have been conducted at Eglin Air Force Base with each type of ordnance noted above. The results were highly satisfactory."

The following week the Air Force request was discussed by the Joint Chiefs. The Air Force Chief of Staff explained that deficiencies in existing ground support aircraft and the absence of new designs under development made it necessary to consider other aircraft types for the ground support mission. He summarized the results of the tests at Eglin Air Force Base and assured his colleagues that the slightly modified F 10B would fulfill the requirements adequately. "It sounds fine to me," said the Army Chief of Staff, "except I would like to have the F 10B equipped to carry the new Bulldog air-to-ground missiles instead of 500-pound bombs.[2] Those 500-pound bombs aren't particularly accurate—why I remember in Korea the Air Force kept my regiment waiting all day while it tried

2. The Bulldog is an air-to-gound guided rocket. It is launched at a range of 4–6 nautical miles from the target, and is guided to the target by the pilot. Although the warhead of the Bulldog is somewhat lighter in weight than the explosive charge in a 500-pound bomb, the two weapons have roughly similar effects on ground targets.

to hit a bridge with 500-pounders. The tactical situations we expect to encounter will not permit delays of that duration or such a degree of inaccuracy."

The Air Staff action officer[3] proceeded to explain that bomb racks and fire control equipment for the Bulldog missile would cost $300,000 per aircraft, as compared with only $25,000 for the corresponding items for 500-pound bombs. He pointed out that it also would be necessary to procure an additional quantity of Bulldogs since relatively few were maintained in stock. At an initial cost of $6,500 each, plus ten-year storage and maintenance costs of $500 per missile, the total ten-year costs were $7,000 per missile. In contrast, a large quantity of 500-pound bombs were already available, left over from World War II and Korea. Relatively simple and easy to maintain, the annual storage and maintenance cost is only $10 per bomb. For these reasons the Air Force recommended that the F 10B be equipped to carry 500-pound bombs rather than Bulldog missiles.

The Army Chief of Staff was not satisfied. "Admittedly, it would be cheaper to use 500-pound bombs. However, the extra cost of equipping the F 10B to carry the Bulldog is not particularly great. Furthermore, we should be buying the Bulldog—it is so much better than bombs. Bombs are not only inaccurate but even during Korea many failed to detonate upon impact." "I agree with the Army," added the Commandant of the Marine Corps. "The attack aircraft assigned to Marine Air Groups are equipped with Bulldogs. It has turned in a most impressive performance in recent maneuvers." The Chairman, who had followed the discussion closely, interrupted: "I suggest we defer the matter until next week. In the meantime I'll have the Joint Staff take a look at the problem."

Student Requirement

You are a member of the Special Studies Group of the Joint Staff. The problem discussed by the Joint Chiefs has been referred to you. Prepare the analysis requested by the Chairman of the Joint Chiefs of Staff, including such recommendations as you deem appropriate.

For the purposes of your analysis, assume the following:

Cost Factors
  Bomb rack and fire-control equipment
    Bulldog $50,000/missile carried
    500# bombs $2,500/bomb carried

---

3. The "action officer" is the officer who has done all the preliminary staff work and coordination on a proposal. When "his" paper is discussed by the Joint Chiefs, the action officer waits in the ante-room of the Joint Chiefs' Conference Room, ready to answer questions or to provide further detail. When the Joint Chiefs discuss problems affecting all the services, an action officer from each service usually will be present.

Ordnance
> Procurement Costs
>> Bulldog $6,500/missile
>> 500# bombs None (sufficient stocks already available)
> Ten-year Storage & Maintenance Costs[4]
>> Bulldog $500/missile
>> 500# bombs $100/bomb

Miscellaneous Factors
> *Single Shot Kill Probabilities*
>> Bulldog .70
>> 500# bomb .32
> Desired confidence level of target destruction—90%
> Duration of average sortie—2 hours
> *F 10B*
>> Cost $2.4 million/aircraft
>> Attack Speed (knots) *Max:* 670; *Min:* 325
>> Estimated aircraft attrition rate in ground support operations—100/10,000 flying hours.
>> Estimated cost/flying hour $800
>> Ordnance Load: 2—20-mm machine gun pods
>>> 8—4″ rockets
>> plus *one* of the following:
>>> 10—500# bombs
>>> 6—napalm containers
>>> 6—Bulldog missiles

Attack Profiles
500-Pound Bombs. Flight to the target area occurs at normal operating altitudes (30-35,000 ft.). Once target is identified, the aircraft dives at the target. Ordnance is released at a slant range (actual distance from aircraft to target) of 2,000 to 1,500 feet. Speed during attack dive is 350-400 knots.

Bulldog. Flight to target area at normal operating altitudes. Once target is identified the aircraft approaches the target in straight and level flight, altitude 5,000-10,000 feet. Ordnance is released at a range of 4-6 nautical miles and guided to the target by pilot. Speed during attack is 650 knots or greater.

---

4. Operation and maintenance costs are calculated on the basis of a ten-year term—the projected utilization period. For most items of military equipment the utilization period is assumed to be five years. For ordnance items, however, storage and maintenance costs are normally calculated over a ten-year period, primarily because ammunition and explosives are both physically easy to store and chemically stable over long periods.

ANALYSIS

MEMORANDUM FOR THE CHAIRMAN
SUBJECT: Ordnance for the F 10B

1. This paper examines the question of external ordnance racks, accessory fire control equipment, and ordnance load for the F 10B, as requested by your memorandum of 16 February.

2. At first glance it seems advisable to accept the Air Force position and equip the F 10B with 500-pound bombs. Procurement and ten-year storage and maintenance costs amount to only $100 for each 500-pound bomb versus $7,000 for each Bulldog. In addition, the ordnance racks for 500-pound bombs are substantially cheaper than those for the Bulldog. On a cost per weapon basis, therefore, the advantage is clearly—indeed overwhelmingly—in favor of 500-pound bombs. However, this simple analysis misses the relevant questions.

3. The reason for procuring the F 10B is to provide additional ground support capability for limited war operations. This capability consists of two compatible but separate components: an aircraft, which transports the ordnance load and fire control equipment to the vicinity of the target, and the ordnance itself. The purpose of this combination of an aircraft and ordnance is to destroy ground targets. The relevant criterion of this or similar weapon systems, therefore, is the cost of destroying an existing ground target.

4. In theory at least it would be desirable to compare alternate combinations of carriers (aircraft) and ordnance items to determine which is most efficient in ground support operations. In this instance a major decision has, at least implicitly, already been agreed to—the F 10B has been selected as the best available aircraft. The question which remains is: With which of two available ordnance loads—Bulldog missiles or 500-pound bombs—should the F 10B be equipped to provide the most economical method of destroying ground targets? It should be noted that putting the question in economic terms, i.e., dollar costs, does not change the problem: it simply makes the obvious assumption that virtually any target could be destroyed by either Bulldogs or bombs.

5. The method employed here is first to determine the number of weapons required to attain a given level of assurance of target destruction. The desired confidence level is 90 percent. We then proceed to calculate the cost of destroying a target using each ordnance item.

a) The number of rounds required to insure target destruction at a given confidence level is computed as follows.

$$P = 1 - (1-k)^n$$

where

P = degree of confidence of target destruction

k = single shot hit probability

n = number of rounds

Bulldog

$$.9 = 1 - (1 - .7)^n$$
$$.9 = 1 - .3^n$$
$$-.3^n = -.1$$
$$n = \frac{\ln .1}{\ln .3}$$

n = 1.9 or 2 missiles/target kill

500 # bomb

$$.9 = 1 - (1 - .32)^n$$
$$.9 = 1 - .68^n$$
$$-.68^n = -.1$$
$$n = \frac{\ln .1}{\ln .68}$$

n = 6 bombs/target kill

b) *Ordnance cost/target kill* (C_o)

cost = number of weapons/target kill $\times$ (procurement cost/weapon + 10 year storage & maintenance costs/weapon)

Bulldog

$$C_o = 2 \times (6,500 + 500)$$
$$C_o = \$14,000/\text{target destroyed}$$

500# bombs

$$C_o = 6 \times (0 + 100)$$
$$C_o = \$600/\text{target destroyed}$$

c) *Cost of delivery per target kill* (C_d)

$$\text{cost of delivery/target kill} = \frac{\text{number of weapons/target kill}}{\text{number of weapons/sortie}}$$

$$\times \text{ average length of sortie in hours} \times \frac{\text{cost}}{\text{flying hour}}$$

Bulldog

$$C_d = 2/6 \times 2 \times 800 = \$533$$

500# bombs

$$C_d = 6/10 \times 2 \times 800 = \$960$$

d) *Attrition costs per target kills* (C_a)

$$\text{attrition costs/target kill} = \frac{\text{flying hours}}{\text{target kill}} \times \text{attrition rate}^a \times \frac{\text{cost}^b}{\text{aircraft}}$$

Bulldog

$$C_a = 2/3 \times .01 \times \$2.7 \text{ million}$$
$$C_a = 2/3 \times 27,000 = \$18,000$$

500# bombs

$$C_a = 6/5 \times .01 \times \$2.425 \text{ million}$$
$$C_a = 1.2 \times 24,250 = \$29,100$$

e) *Costs/target destroyed*

$$C_{TD} = C_o + C_d + C_a$$

Bulldog

$C_o =$	$14,000
$C_d =$	533
$C_a =$	18,000
	$32,533

500# bombs

$C_o =$	$ 600
$C_d =$	960
$C_a =$	29,100
	$30,660

a. Attrition rate is 100 aircraft/10,000 flying hours or .01.

b. The cost/aircraft is $2.4 million. To this figure must be added the costs of the external racks and fire control equipment associated with each type of ordnance—$300,000 for Bulldogs and $25,000 for bombs. The cost/aircraft with Bulldog is thus $2.7 million; an aircraft equipped with 500# bombs will cost $2.425 million.

6. On the basis of the criterion—costs per target kill—500# bombs provide the least cost solution. To destroy a target with Bulldogs will cost approximately $1,870 more than with 500# bombs.

7. *Other Considerations.* There are several major qualitative differences between these ordnance items. First, supported ground forces prefer Bulldog. Its greater accuracy means that ground units will spend less time under fire, waiting for friendly aircraft to attack and destroy hostile targets. As a result a reduction in Army casualties may reasonably be expected by the use of Bulldog. Further, more rapid destruction of enemy forces will speed up the ground battle, also to the advantage of U.S. forces.

Second, if the force is equipped with Bulldog it will be able to attack a substantially greater number of targets in any given period of time. For example, assume an eight squadron force, flying one sortie per day, with an aircraft availability rate of 80 percent. If armed with Bulldog, this force could attack and destroy nearly 1,400 ground targets in a three-day period. If equipped with 500-pound bombs, 768 targets—only 55 percent as many—could be destroyed.[5] Although there is no way of knowing the number of targets which might be presented during a particular operation, tactical squadrons equipped with Bulldog have a markedly enhanced target kill capability within a given time period. This capability is likely to be particularly important during the initial stages of a limited conflict, when the number of U.S. aircraft is small and the number of targets relatively large.

A final consideration is pilot losses. The Bulldog is fired at a range of 4-6 miles from the target with the aircraft at an altitude of 5,000 to 10,000 feet—beyond the range of small arms fire. In a bombing attack, in contrast, the pilot dives at the target, releasing his ordnance at a slant range of 1,500 to 2,000 feet—well within the range of local antiaircraft defensive weapons. Therefore, aircraft equipped with Bulldog will normally be exposed to enemy ground fire for a shorter period of time than aircraft carrying 500# bombs. For this reason pilot losses may be expected to be lower with the Bulldog.[6]

The Bulldog thus provides three major advantages—reduced ground force casualties, an increased target kill potential, and lower pilot losses—which would not be present were the force equipped with 500# bombs. Since the Bulldog costs

5. Determined as follows:

$$\frac{\text{Targets destroyed}}{\text{period}} = \text{total number of aircraft in force} \times \text{availability}$$

$$\text{rate} \times \frac{\text{sorties}}{\text{day}} \times \frac{\text{days}}{\text{period}} \times \frac{\text{target kills}}{\text{sortie}}$$

Bulldog	*500# bombs*
TD = 192 × .8 × 1 × 3 × 3	TD = 192 × .8 × 1 × 3 × 1.67
TD = 1,382	TD = 768

6. The problem of pilot losses can be treated *quantitatively,* rather than *qualitatively.* This does not necessarily require the analyst to put a price tag on human life; it does, however, require computation of the *costs of training a replacement pilot.*

approximately $1,870 more per target destroyed, these qualitative advantages must be weighed against the additional cost which will be incurred. Put in other terms, are lower casualties and increased target kill potential worth the additional costs? In the opinion of the undersigned, the additional qualitative advantages more than offset the extra costs.

To suggest that pilot losses will be lower with Bulldog is tantamount to saying that the attrition rate of a force equipped with Bulldogs is lower than the rate experienced by a force equipped with 500# bombs. The problem of attrition rates is also discussed in the Concluding Comments.

8. *Recommendation.* Procure the Bulldog missiles for the eight squadron force proposed by the Air Force.

9. *Questions for Further Study.* Some types of targets, troops in the open for example, are most easily destroyed with weapons other than the Bulldog. There are two possible ways to provide this capability: (1) equip a small number of aircraft with external racks for 500-pound bombs and napalm containers; or (2) develop a modified external ordnance rack compatible with all major bombs and missiles. The second alternative should be given careful consideration, since it allows local commanders more flexibility than the first.

/s/

Commander, USN

COMMENTS ON THIS ANALYSIS

Several aspects of the analysis have been simplified to reduce the complexity of the computations. These include:

1. Sortie duration varies from theater to theater, depending on base location, target location, and the pattern of enemy air defenses. The assumed two-hour sortie duration greatly simplifies the calculations.

2. The actual computation of aircraft losses is more complicated than the method employed in this problem. Briefly, there are two ways to estimate aircraft losses: First, losses may be calculated on a "5-1-1/2" basis (if the operations area is heavily defended, the factors may be increased to "10-2-1")—5 percent of the force per sortie lost during the first three days of operations, 1 percent per sortie during the remainder of the first 60 days, and 1/2 percent per sortie thereafter. Another method is to use differential loss rates, one rate for the time aircraft are flying in the target area (where the aircraft encounters defensive fires) and a lower rate for the time spent en route to and from the target areas. The rates mentioned above are based on the attrition patterns of World War II and Korea. Some analysts believe that improved air defense systems, such as are found in Europe, would lead to losses as high as 25-50 percent per sortie. In that event there would be no force to speak of after three days.

3. The solution to this problem is highly sensitive to attrition rates. As illustrated in Graph I, below, with a rate of .0117 (117 aircraft lost per 10,000 flying hours) the costs per target kill are identical.[7] Above that point, the Bulldog always costs less; below, the cost advantages fall to 500# bombs. And if, as suggested in paragraph 7 and footnote #6, there is any substantial difference in the rates of the two systems, the Bulldog may well provide the least cost solution. For example, if the attrition rate for Bulldog is .008 (80 planes per 10,000 flying hours), as compared to .01 for 500# bombs, the Bulldog will cost less per target kill.

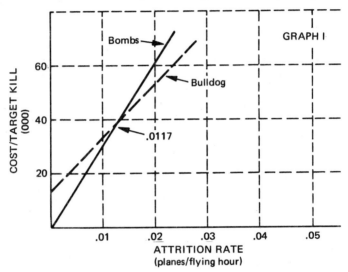

7. Attrition costs per target kill are a linear function of the attrition rate. To determine that attrition rate at which the two systems will have identical costs it is necessary simply to equate the two equations for total costs per target destroyed and then solve for the attrition rate (r_a). Thus

Bulldog

$C_{TD} = C_o + C_d + C_a$
$C_{TD} = \$14{,}000 + \$533 + C_a$
$C_{TD} = \$14{,}533 + C_a$

But

$C_a = \$1{,}800{,}000 \times r_a$

Substituting:

$C_{TD} = \$14{,}533 + \$1.8 \times 10^6 \times r_a$

500# bombs

$C_{TD} = C_o + C_d + C_a$
$C_{TD} = \$600 + \$960 + C_a$
$C_{TD} = \$1{,}560 + C_a$

$C_a = \$2{,}910{,}000 \times r_a$

$C_{TD} = \$1{,}560 + \$2.9 \times 10^6 \times r_a$

Since C_{TD} is assumed to be the same, the two equations may be equated:

$\$14{,}533 + \$1.8 \times 10^6 \times r_a = \$1{,}560 + \$2.9 \times 10^6 \times r_a$
$(\$2.9 \times 10^6 \times r_a) - (\$1.8 \times 10^6 \times r_a) = \$14{,}533 - \$1{,}560$
$\$1.1 \times 10^6 \times r_a = \$12{,}973$

$$r_a = \frac{12973}{1.1} \times 10^{-6}$$

$$r_a = .0117$$

Therefore, at this rate (117 aircraft lost per 10,000 flying hours) the costs per target destroyed are the same for the two systems.

4. The confidence level (90 percent) of target destruction is unusually high. A more realistic level would be 80-85 percent. A thorough analysis would vary confidence levels to determine the sensitivity of the problem to changes in this assumption. (A preliminary analysis suggests that the solution would not change.)

5. An approximate method for including the costs of pilot losses is to: (1) assume the pilot is lost each time an aircraft is destroyed; (2) add the costs of training a pilot to the capital costs of the system, i.e., aircraft costs plus the costs of associated ordnance racks and fire control equipment. Therefore, if it costs $100,000 to train a pilot, the attrition costs using Bulldog is increased to $18,667; using 500# bombs, C_a jumps to $30,300. Consideration of this additional cost thus further narrows the already slight economic advantage of 500# bombs. If replacement training were much in excess of $300,000 per pilot, the Bulldog would then be the least costly system in terms of costs per target kill.

Concluding Comments

To date, much of the work in systems analysis has been concerned with comparisons of weapon systems. "Bomb Racks for the F 10B" is a relatively straightforward comparison of two systems, and illustrates some of the techniques which are useful in analyses of this type.

In general terms, there are two ways in which systems can be compared: (1) Fix a level of performance, and then determine how much it costs for each system to meet this standard. Other things being equal, the least-cost system is preferred. (2) Assume that an equal quantity of resources is available for investment in each system and then determine which system provides the greatest output. The two approaches, in short, are "equal effectiveness, varying costs"; and "equal costs, varying effectiveness." The first method of comparison is generally the easiest to handle, and was the method employed in the analysis of ordnance requirements for the F 10B.

Whatever the approach, a vital first step is to select a criterion, that is, a measure of effectiveness. In other words, what are the systems designed to do?—and what kind of yardsticks are appropriate measures of this performance? "Bomb Racks for the F 10B" is an excellent illustration of the difficulties involved in criterion selection, and of the consequences of an improper choice.

The original proposal to use 500# bombs failed to specify the criterion upon which the Air Force's choice was based. Since bombs are less expensive than Bulldogs, the implicit criterion would seem to be costs per unit of ordnance. This criterion assumes that the two items of ordnance are equally effective against ground targets. If either weapon hits a target, it will be destroyed; the chances of hitting a target, however, are by no means the same. The bomb and Bulldog, therefore, are not equally effective, and a comparison of their costs is inconclusive. It would appear that the analyst was so impressed by the gross differences in ordnance costs that he failed to consider the costs of the other components of the system. Nevertheless, units of ordnance are simply *inputs* into the system—as pointed out in the "Analysis," both ordnance and aircraft are required to do the job.

The criterion employed in the "Analysis" is costs per target kill. This is an appropriate criterion in that it is concerned with the principal military task of the weapon system. Determining the costs per target kill requires the analyst to determine not only ordnance costs but the costs of flying and attrition. As it turns out, these costs are substantially greater than ordnance costs—witness the dramatic change in outcome of the analysis.

When the systems are compared in terms of the new criterion, the differences in cost are small—rather than overwhelmingly in favor of 500# bombs. Indeed, the difference between the two systems is now such a small percentage of the overall costs that the decision maker should ignore costs and base his choice upon the qualitative features of the two systems. The reason, of course, is that the cost data employed in the analysis are simply a best estimate, and are likely to change over the life of the system. It is thus inadvisable to attach too much significance to relatively minor differences, in either costs or performance.

The point is sufficiently important to warrant a more general observation. The quantitative methods, models, and explicit assumptions which *should* characterize systems analysis often tend to create a sense of precision and accuracy. More often than not, this sense of precision is unwarranted—almost all of the relevant variables in an analysis involve some degree of uncertainty, and it is highly probable that the numbers employed in the analysis will differ somewhat from their actual value. In some instances, the variance is sufficiently important to cause a major change in the outcome of the problem. Hence, experienced analysts—and users of analyses—quite properly view the results with caution. If the costs or performance of the alternatives are substantially different, other things being equal, there is little difficulty in choosing. When the differences are minor, the choice requires careful consideration, particularly of the uncertainties which are involved. In short, it is important to exercise judgment in the interpretation of the results—and not be carried away by the analysis itself.

"Bomb Racks for the F 10B" also illustrates a technique known to analysts as "sensitivity analysis." In this particular case there are a number of variables relevant to the analysis. Aircraft costs, sortie duration, and ordnance load are examples. Not all of the variables are of equal importance, however. Cost computations indicate the contribution made by each variable to overall costs per target kill. Since attrition costs account for two-thirds or more of total costs, the analysts should give careful attention to the data and the assumptions about this factor. In so doing, it is readily apparent that the indicated attrition rate (100 aircraft lost per 100,000 flying hours) is only an estimate. It is, moreover, an estimate shot through with uncertainties, and the rate might vary considerably under different tactical conditions. The analyst, therefore, will want to find out how the solution to the problem will be affected if the attrition rate were at some other level. This sensitivity analysis is conducted in paragraph 3 of the

"Comments." The point is that in any analysis some factors are more important than others. In addition, the degree of uncertainty inherent in each variable is different. It is necessary to seek out these critical variables, to see how sensitive the outcome is to them, and then to make a judgment about them—are they likely to change and, if so, in what way?

Sensitivity analysis is closely related to the question of judgment and experience and their proper roles in decision making. The purpose of systems analysis is to solve the easier parts of the problem, and thereby provide decision makers an opportunity to focus their attention on those aspects which require the exercise of judgment. Having determined that attrition rate is both a key and an uncertain variable, the decision maker may well decide that this question is of sufficient importance to warrant additional consideration. Certainly he will want the advice and judgment of others—not only officers with relevant military experience, but also knowledgeable engineers and scientists. If advisers are of the opinion that the attrition rate will differ materially from the level assumed by the analyst, the revised data must be utilized in the computations. If sensitivity analysis has been employed, the effect of the change is already known, and a decision can be made. This technique, in short, helps to highlight those critical and uncertain elements of the problem in which experience, intuition, and judgment are the proper bases for decision.

"Bomb Racks for the F 10B" also suggests that one of the major advantages of systems analysis is the new ideas it generates. The important new idea is the proposal that aircraft external racks be made compatible with all types of ordnance items. Clearly, the idea is worth exploring—and it would be possible to do so without great difficulty. Would it have been proposed without the extensive analysis that went into the problem?

Part Three: Analytic Examples

This part contains four completed analytic studies illustrating different types of analysis.

The first example presents an analysis of fireboat deployment in New York harbor, which utilizes a uniquely simple simulation method to reduce the cost of maintaining the same level of effectiveness.

The second example employs a broad systems approach in examining public and private services to the blind.

The third example presents a benefit-cost analysis of a proposed program to reduce migration of businesses from New York City by using the city's urban renewal powers to assemble small industrial sites.

The fourth example employs a computer simulation model to analyze alternative methods of reducing delays in processing felonies in the District of Columbia.

Fireboat Deployment in New York Harbor

INTRODUCTION

This report[1] presents an analysis of various possible deployments of the New York Fire Department's fireboat fleet–i.e., various possible patterns of locating marine companies around the waterfront, and various sizes of the fleet.

Marine company activities (number of incidents involving the department's fireboats) have been declining steadily over the past few years. In 1967, average actual fire duty per company was only one-third the 1965 level. This suggested the desirability of examining whether the existing fleet of eight large fireboats is still needed to provide adequate protection to the harbor area, and whether the existing location of fireboats is optimal given the historical geographical pattern of fires.

Measuring "adequate protection" is, clearly, a difficult task. It is therefore necessary to select a measure which can be used as a substitute or proxy for protection. The measure selected is "response time." This choice was based on the notion that the sooner a fireboat arrives at the scene of the incident, the sooner the fire can be brought under control. There is no data available to relate reduced response times with, for example, reduced fire damage; however, it appears to be intuitively obvious that they are related. Accordingly, response time was selected as a proxy for protection capability; it is used in the following analysis as a numerical measure to compare marginal changes in the protection capability resulting from variations in the size and location of the fireboat fleet.

Historical records (1965, 1966, and 1967) were examined, and the locations of incidents involving each fireboat were plotted on a map of New York harbor. For each of the alternate deployments considered (various sizes and locations of the fleet), the percentages of incidents which occurred within six minutes' and twelve minutes' travel time of each fireboat berth were counted. Analysis of these data led to the following conclusions:

1. One fireboat company (Marine 7) should be immediately abandoned; the fireboat itself should, however, be kept as a spare boat (saving approximately $700,000 annually).

2. Subsequently, Marine 1 could be abandoned without a major decrease in fire protection capability. More efficient operation would be achieved if Marine 5 were consolidated with Marine 4 and relocated more centrally; a small seasonal unit would cover the outer reaches of the East River during the boating season (saving approximately $1,400,000 annually).

---

1. This example was prepared by Graeme Taylor, based on original work done by R. Feeley of the Budget Bureau, city of New York.

The Marine Division

The Marine Division of the New York Fire Department maintains eight large fireboats for the purpose of fighting ship and waterfront fires; secondary duties of the Marine Division include (*a*) provision of additional manpower for fighting land fires near the waterfront (*b*) elimination of waterfront fire hazards through a pier inspection program (*c*) search and rescue work in the vicinity of fireboat berths (*d*) securing barges that may go adrift and (*e*) washing down oil spills to remove potential fire hazards.

Approximately six times per year, incidents occur where two or more fireboats are used. Occasionally, the extra boats assigned are not actually used; for example, in the *Manchester Miller* fire, three boats were assigned, but only two were able to position themselves to supply the hose lines. A few major disasters, such as the *Alva Cape* explosion of June, 1966, have actually utilized more than two boats. In the majority of instances, therefore, only one fireboat is deployed per incident. However, the need to respond to occasional major disasters sets a minimum size for the fleet.

The fireboat has two unique attributes of importance in fighting fires. First, because it is a boat, it can supply men and water to positions inaccessible to land fire companies, including the seaward faces of docks, ships at anchor, at piers, or under way, and islands or installations remote from land. In addition, the fireboat can deliver large volumes of water (5,000–20,000 gallons per minute) at high pressures directly from the harbor onto the fire, and is thus independent of the water mains as a source of supply.[2]

Marine company activities have been declining steadily over the past few years. This is in part due to the changing character of the waterfront, particularly the demolition and reconstruction of piers, and in part to a more effective prevention campaign. In 1965, actual fire duty averaged approximately 80 hours per company; by 1967, this had declined to approximately 27 hours per company.

The cruising speed of existing New York fireboats is twelve knots, but adverse currents may reduce this by two to three knots. New York's eight fireboats range in age from eight to thirty-eight years. The crew of each vessel averages ten to eleven men including a pilot, fire company officer, two to four marine engineers and "wipers" (engine maintenance men), and five or six firemen. Since these posts are manned twenty-four hours per day, the necessary complement for a marine fire company is about fifty men. Thus, estimated full costs for one marine fire company are approximately $900,000 per year. (It is estimated that the marginal cost of one marine company is approximately $700,000 per year;

---

2. The recent introduction of the Super Pumper System does provide on land the capability to supply water at high pressures and volumes from an independent source. The Super Pumper is mounted on a large trailer truck, and can be transported anywhere in the city at high speed.

i.e., approximately $700,000 could be saved annually if one marine company is eliminated.)

Table 1
Estimated Costs for the Marine Division

Personal services	$4,990,000
Allowance for impact of new contract now in collective bargaining	500,000
Estimated fringe benefits (30%)	1,650,000
Supplies and maintenance	100,000
Total	$7,240,000

Brief descriptions of each of the eight fireboat companies are presented in Appendix I at the end of this paper.

FRAMEWORK OF ANALYSIS

The analysis was performed in four stages as follows:
1. A record of incidents at which fireboats actually worked was compiled for the years 1965, 1966, and 1967.
2. The numbers of incidents and hours of fire duty were plotted by location on a map of New York harbor.
3. Four alternative deployments of the fireboat fleet were selected for analysis.
4. For each alternative, the number of incidents that occurred within (*a*) one mile and (*b*) two miles of each fireboat berth was measured. (Distances were measured along navigable waterways.)

This analysis resulted in a summary table (Table 3) which displayed the percentage of incidents that occurred within travel times of (*a*) six minutes and (*b*) twelve minutes of a fireboat berth—for each of the four deployments analyzed. This table was then used as the basis for judgments as to the relative adequacy of protection afforded by each alternative.

It should be emphasized that the measure of "protection capability" used in this analysis is "response time." A deployment alternative which placed fireboat berths near a high percentage of incidents is therefore considered better than a deployment alternative where fireboat berths were located near a lower percentage of incidents.

Response time is, of course, only a proxy for "protection." No information presently exists on the connection between "protection" and the time a fireboat takes to reach the fire. Presumably it is more desirable for a fireboat to be able to reach a fire in six minutes than in sixty minutes, but it is impossible to say *how much more desirable.* This area deserves further study. In the meantime, given the present size and location of the fleet, six minutes and twelve minutes appeared to be reasonable reference times to use in the analysis.

Incident Data

Activity levels as reported by the Marine Division include fires and other emergencies for which the unique attributes of fireboats are not essential. For 1967, the Marine Division reported 3,276 responses, 260 "workers" (incidents where a fireboat was actually used), and 512 hours of working time (including travel to and from the incident). Therefore, the eight fireboat companies each averaged little more than one response per day, 2.5 workers per month, and 64 hours of work per year. Many land fire companies, by contrast, average over ten responses per day and 1,000 hours of work per year.

The first task was to refine the above data by compiling a record of actual fire incidents at which fireboats worked. The records of each fireboat company for the years 1965, 1966, and 1967 were accordingly examined. All fires at which a fireboat actually worked were recorded, along with the location of the incident, the number of work hours, and the number of marine companies actually used at the fire. In addition to fires, the tabulation included incidents of oil spills where fireboat pumps were used to wash down a fire hazard. Responses excluded from the tabulation consisted of fires where the crew responded on foot, false alarms, responses where a fireboat was not needed, and emergencies which were not the primary responsibility of a fireboat.

The incident data used in this analysis are shown in Table 2.

Table 2
Modified Marine Company Incident Data 1965-1967

Marine Company Number	Number of Incidents			Hours Worked		
	1965	*1966*	*1967*	*1965*	*1966*	*1967*
1	14	17	13	45.67	33.58	22.08
2	23	26	23	67.00	45.50	40.92
4	24	21	13	41.25	55.67	55.17
5	27	22	7	38.08	27.25	16.58
6	20	18	15	96.58	55.00	16.00
7	18	20	9	127.17	32.08	18.00
8	42	31	21	103.00	88.00	24.17
9	42	42	13	120.75	114.92	21.67
Total	210	197	114	639.50	452.00	214.59

Plotting the Data

On a map of New York harbor, two numbers were plotted for each alarm box position or specific fire site—the total number of incidents and the total number of fireboat company hours worked at that location during the three-year period.

Selection of Alternative Deployments for Analysis

Four possible deployments of the fireboat fleet were examined:
1. The existing fleet, with the berths as presently assigned.
2. The existing fleet, but with the *addition* of the previously abandoned Marine Company No. 3.
3. The existing fleet, *minus* two fireboats—Marine 1 (Battery Park) and Marine 7 (Fulton Street in Brooklyn).
4. The existing fleet, *minus* Marine 7, and *relocation* of Marine 1 to the Fulton Street site.

Response Analysis

For each of the four alternative deployments considered, the number of incidents within one nautical mile and within two nautical miles of a fireboat berth were counted. In view of the complex geography of New York harbor, this was accomplished from the incident map using a piece of string as the measuring device.[3] Assuming a uniform speed of 10 knots, incidents within one nautical mile of a berth would have a boat available within six minutes, and incidents within two nautical miles would have a boat available in twelve minutes. The results are given in Table 3.

Commentary on Table 3

It can be noted that the incremental protection which would have been provided by another fireboat company (Marine 3 on West 52nd Street) is very low. Only 41.6 percent of all incidents would have had boats available within six minutes, while 40 percent had the same protection with only eight boats. The difference in twelve-minute coverage is even less—62.0 percent of all incidents with nine boats, 61.6 percent of all incidents with eight boats.

The loss of protection under alternative 4 is also remarkably small. With the reduced fleet, 60.5 percent of all incidents have a boat available within twelve minutes. An additional 1.1 percent of all incidents and 3.2 percent of working hours would then be outside a two-mile zone of protection. (Every one of these

---

3. String was used so that distances could be "bent" around the irregular geography of New York harbor.

incidents with decreased fire protection is on the New Jersey shore—an area not the direct responsibility of the New York Fire Department.)

Table 3
Response Analysis for Alternative Deployments

	Six-Minute Coverage (1 Mile)				Twelve-Minute Coverage (2 Miles)			
	Incidents		Hours Worked		Incidents		Hours Worked	
Alternative	*No.*	*%*	*Hrs.*	*%*	*No.*	*%*	*Hrs.*	*%*
1. Existing fleet	198	40.0	350.9	36.7	306	61.6	606.6	58.6
2. Add Marine 3	206	41.6	392.8	37.9	308	62.0	619.5	59.5
3. Eliminate Marine 1 and 7	153	30.9	246.1	23.8	282	57.0	525.4	50.7
4. Eliminate Marine 7, move 1 to Fulton St.	171	34.5	264.5	25.6	300	60.5	573.7	55.4

The loss of two boats in the central harbor area (alternative 3) would cause a notable change in incidents covered within one mile. The percentage of incidents covered falls from 40.0 to 30.9 percent, and the percentage of work hours from 36.7 to 23.8 percent. If one considers two-mile (twelve-minute) coverage, however, the loss of two boats does not result in such a major reduction in incidents covered—57.0 percent as compared with 61.6 percent. (Once again, a number of these incidents are on the Jersey shore.)

The loss of one marine unit in the central harbor area, therefore, would create relatively little change in the pattern of coverage for fire incidents which occurred in the recent past, particularly in the two mile coverage zone. Discontinuing two units has a greater effect, but still far less in proportion to previous performance than the resulting decrease in cost ($1,400,000, or 20 percent). The probability of simultaneous incidents is so low, because of their infrequency, that it is unlikely that a boat would not be available to these incidents as indicated. However, it would be advisable to maintain an extra fireboat without crew, so that no marine company need be out of service while its vessel is being repaired.

Analysis of the Outer Harbor

Alternative deployments for fireboats in the outer harbor area were not considered in a manner similar to that described above for the inner harbor. However, reference to Table 2 and the incident map suggested the following analysis.

Though the number of hours of work performed by Marine 4 has remained relatively constant and about average for the fireboat fleet, the unit is poorly situated in relation to the demand for its services. Furthermore, the demands on this unit are extremely seasonal. During the five winter months of 1965 (January, February, March, November and December), this unit had only six fire incidents. In 1966, there were only two incidents during these months, and three incidents during the same period in 1967. The department might consider a seasonal assignment at Fort Totten on City Island of *Smoke II,* equipped with a somewhat larger fire pump. This vessel could then handle small pier and pleasure boat fires, and be used as a command boat during the five winter months. Since many of the major fires where Marine 4 operated are further down the East River from Fort Totten, or up Westchester Creek, this big fireboat might then be berthed at a point near Rikers Island. Because of its 20-knot speed, the maximum delay in reaching major fires on City Island or in the Pelham Bay area would be twelve minutes (four miles), when compared with the present position at Fort Totten.

By positioning Marine 4 near Rikers Island, Marine 5 might then be eliminated. This unit had a substantial number of small fires near its base, many of which might have been extinguished by land companies. Downriver from Marine 5, as far as the Newtown Creek area, there were practically no fire incidents. A repositioned Marine 4 might be as much as ten to twelve minutes later in reaching Harlem River fires, but any company is delayed substantially by the bridges on this waterway. Low and declining activity levels for Marine 5—seven incidents and 16.5 work hours in 1967—dictate serious consideration of this consolidation, with a seasonal company in a small, fast fire launch on the outer reaches of the East River.

In 1965, Marine Companies 8 and 9 were the busiest in New York, with more than 40 incidents and over 100 working hours. In 1967, this situation had changed, and Marine 9 had only 13 incidents and 22 hours of work time. In addition, the incidents handled by Marine 9 are often at a substantial distance from its base along the Arthur Kill or Kill Van Kull. If Marine 8 were to cover this area, it would be 2.5 miles, or 15 minutes, further away from any Staten Island incident. If the marine Division is to consider increasing the speed of its units, the Staten Island area would benefit most from this program, and Marine Units 8 and 9 might ultimately be consolidated.

CONCLUSIONS AND RECOMMENDATIONS

The *immediate* abandonment of one company (Marine 7) should be effected. The marginal fire protection provided by this unit is low. In fact, this unit has not been fully manned for several months. However, the fireboat itself should be maintained. By maintaining a spare vessel, we can assure that the budgeted number of marine companies will always be available, because the spare boat can be substituted when another vessel is out of service. Since the positions for the crew of this unit are largely vacant, the reduction of one marine company can be effected without major personnel dislocations. The budgetary saving from this reduction, without a reduction in overhead or boat maintenance, should be about $700,000 per year. If necessary, one or two men could be retained to perform, by car or launch, the inspection program carried on by Marine 7.

Stage two of a marine consolidation program could discontinue Marine Company 1. As shown in the analysis, the marginal protection provided for recent incidents by Marine 1 and Marine 7 was relatively small. At the same time, the consolidation of Marine 4 and 5 into the high speed unit *John H. Glenn,* located in a more central position, should be considered. A small seasonal unit would cover the outer reaches of the East River during the boating season. Additional savings are estimated at $1,400,000 per year.

A third stage would envision one high-speed, high capacity fireboat to replace Marine 8 and 9, for additional savings of $700,000 per year.

As pointed out above, very few incidents occur requiring the presence of more than one fireboat. The above recommendations, if implemented, would still leave four boats within the area from midtown Manhattan to the Narrows; therefore, at least three boats would be available for any disaster in the central harbor area within 30–45 minutes.

Proposal for Further Analysis

1. This analysis has used the approximate figure of $700,000 as the marginal cost of one fireboat company. Further analysis would refine this estimate to obtain the actual marginal cost of each individual fireboat company.
2. Options for redeployment in the Outer Harbor area described above should be evaluated by the same technique as used for the four Inner Harbor alternatives.
3. More alternate deployments should be studied in order to determine the most effective locations for fireboats for each possible size of the fireboat fleet. The advantages of using some higher-speed fireboats should also be evaluated.
3. Analysis should be performed of the relation between response time and "protection."

APPENDIX I

SUMMARY: NEW YORK MARINE FIRE COMPANIES

Marine 1
Pier A, North River, Manhattan; built 1954; 335 gross tons; 12 mph; pumps 19,000 gallons per minute (GPM) at 150 lbs. pressure

Marine 2
Bloomfield Street, North River, Manhattan; 1931; 269 gross tons; 17 mph; 16,000 GPM at 150 lbs.

Marine 4
Fort Totten, Queens; 1961; 82 gross tons; 20 mph; 5,000 GPM at 150 lbs.

Marine 5
East 90th Street, East River, Manhattan; 1959; 213 gross tons; 8,000 GPM at 150 lbs.

Marine 6
Grand Street, East River, Manhattan; 1958; 213 gross tons; 8,000 GPM at 150 lbs.

Marine 7
Cadman Plaza West; 1958; 213 gross tons; 8,000 GPM at 150 lbs.

Marine 8
52nd Street, Brooklyn; 1961; 213 gross tons; 8,000 GPM at 150 lbs.

Marine 9
St. George Ferry Terminal, Staten Island; 1938; 324 gross tons; 20,000 GPM at 150 lbs.

The Blindness System

INTRODUCTION

As we have become more concerned with the adequacy of our social services—particularly those affecting the poor, the disabled, and the neglected—we have begun to learn not only how hard it is to change inadequate service systems but also how difficult it can be to understand them in the first place. One cluster of approaches to such understanding and such change is that of systems analysis. In these pages, my purpose will be to explore some of the insights one form of systems analysis offers into the complex of institutions which provide services to the blind in the United States.[1]

There exists in this country a "blindness system." By blindness system I mean that interrelated network of people, organizations, rules, and activities which includes: (1) *all persons with severe visual impairments;* (2) *all agencies and groups that serve these people;* (3) *the training and research that affect these services;* (4) *the laws and policies under which services are provided.* To call all this a system is not to imply that it has well-defined, agreed-upon goals and coordinated programs for reaching them. In fact, the complex of institutions is fragmented and tends to behave in a disorganized way. In this sense, it is a *non*system. Nevertheless, all the components listed above affect the experience of the American blind, and we can profit from an examination of the actual *non*system from the point of view of an ideal hypothetical system which *would* arrange its activities and allocate its resources in order to meet its goals in a coordinated way.[2]

Chart I suggests something of the makeup of the actual blindness system in the United States. It estimates the total allocation of dollars to blindness as of 1966 (about $446 million), and indicates the relative contributions to that sum from federal, state, and private sources. It also shows the principal services offered by agencies for the blind. The chart presents the blindness system as a kind of

1. This analytic example was written by Donald A. Schon, president of the Organization for Social and Technical Innovation. It first appeared in the Winter 1970 issue of *The Public Interest;* it is reproduced by permission.

It is based on a year-long study of services to the blind in the United States which was undertaken by the Organization for Social and Technical Innovation in Cambridge, Massachusetts (OSTI), under the sponsorship of the National Institute of Neurological Diseases and Blindness (NINDB). The NINDB is not responsible for the findings and interpretations here.

2. Robert A. Scott's recent study, *The Making of Blind Men,* (NY: Russell Sage Foundation, 1969) is a penetrating analysis of the "blindness system," and I should like to take this opportunity to acknowledge my indebtedness to it.

Chart 1
National resource flows related to blindness

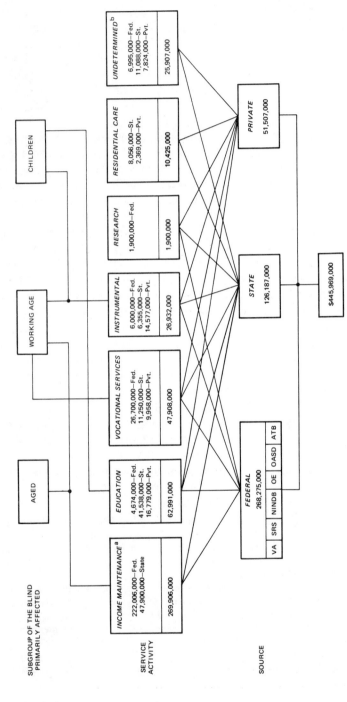

a. This figure includes 118,130,000 of Veterans Administration funds which are allocated on the basis of visual impairment and are not limited to legal blindness.

b. This category includes funds which could not be assigned with confidence to any other service category.

mechanism through which dollars flow from federal, state, and private sources into a variety of service activities which are "matched," in turn, with different categories of blind persons.

Agencies specifically concerned with the blind exist at the federal, state, and local levels. They fall into two parallel systems, one public and the other private—although the clarity of this distinction has been eroded in recent years as private agencies have sought and received greater amounts of public funds. *There are, in all, approximately 800 agencies for the blind,* both public and private. These differ with respect to the services they provide and the basis on which they are organized. Some are specialized in individual functions, such as Aid to the Needy Blind or residential schools for the blind. Others are large, multifunctional agencies. Still others are consulting agencies or producers and distributors of materials for the blind. In addition to the providers of services, there are special organizations concerned with blindness-related research, both medical and nonmedical, and with manpower training. All these constitute what I will call the *official* blindness system, which provides services specifically to the blind.

Beyond that there is an *indirect* system which provides benefits or services to the blind under headings other than blindness, such as welfare, social security, veterans' benefits, and health. The magnitude of this indirect system is substantial. Conservative estimates of the cost of medical and personal care provided to blind persons in general hospitals and nursing homes in 1966 exceed $200 million.

And finally there is an *informal* blindness system, which consists of services to the blind provided not by established agencies, but by families, friends, and neighborhood acquaintances. We have attempted no estimate of the dollar value of these services, but their magnitude—for reasons to be suggested later—may well exceed the entire agency system concerned with the blind.

THE PROBLEM OF DATA

The available data concerning blindness in the United States are exceedingly poor—so poor, in fact, that no significant quantitative statement about the system can be made with any high degree of certainty. Consider, for example, the central question of how many blind people there are. At the present time, there are three principal estimates—see Table 1.

Table 1
Estimated Number of Blind Persons in U.S.

Source	Rate per 1000 population	Total United States
MRA Projection to Total (1965)	1.5	290,000
NSPB Fact Book (1965)	2.1	416,000
National Health Survey	5.6	1,090,000

Of the three estimates, the highest is more than 3 times the lowest. These wide variations exist because different agencies use different definitions of blindness, different test methods, and different sampling procedures.[3]

The Model Reporting Areas (MRA) are 14 associated states which maintain registers of persons with severe vision impairment. They define blindness as "visual acuity of 20/200, if the widest diameter of the field of vision subtends an angle no greater than 20°." This is a variant of the standard accepted definition of "legal blindness." The MRA reporting system requires that persons be listed as blind by an ophthalmologist using the standard Snellen charts.[4] There is reason to believe, however, that ophthalmologists underreport blindness: first, by failing to report as blind, persons (often relatively well-to-do) who wish to avoid the stigma of blindness; and second, because many poor and black persons who are legally blind never go to an ophthalmologist.

The second estimate—that in the Fact Book of the National Society for the Prevention of Blindness (NSPB)—is based on an extrapolation from state demographic data using arbitrary weighting factors tied to the number of people in the blindness register in the state of North Carolina.

The National Health Survey derives its data from household interviews with a sample of the civilian noninstitutionalized population of the United States. It employs no test of visual acuity and classifies persons into groups of severe visual impairment according to the respondent's reply.

Nevertheless, the data concerning the numbers of the blind are actually rather better than those concerning the effect or cost of services provided to the blind, or the number of blind persons receiving benefits from agencies not considered blindness agencies. Some of this information is literally impossible to obtain because of the organization, format, or confidentiality of agency reporting systems. This is another reason why it is difficult to describe, much less evaluate, the blindness system.

3. In my experience, such a state of the data is the norm rather than the exception. That is, the situation with respect to data on blindness does not seem very different from that of other social or medical problems. The statistics on crime, for example, or on the disabilities of children, or on the numbers of the mentally ill are similarly divergent, vague, and fragmentary. In each such instance, the data often say more about the reporting systems than about the problems reported. Police Commissioner Leary, for example, is said to have doubled the crime rate of New York City in one year by enforcing a more stringent reporting of crimes. The state of Kansas was able to "increase" the turnover rate in its mental hospitals by confining old patients to facilities classified as geriatric rather than as hospitals for the mentally ill.

4. Even when the standard Snellen charts are used, serious questions of methodology arise. The Snellen chart lacks fine graduations between 20/100 and 20/200, yet this range is the most critical from the standpoint of classification. (Anyone whose visual acuity is less than 20/100 gets tested next at 20/200.) Moreover, the Snellen chart measures only distance vision; it does not test near vision, which is a better criterion of visual ability. It also does not measure other components of visual performance, such as uniformity of field. Taken by itself, the Snellen chart indicates mainly the ability to read a Snellen chart: it does not indicate whether the subject has useful travel vision, reading vision, or other visual capabilities.

A conspiratorial mind might construe this state of affairs as a defense mechanism adopted by the *non*system as a safeguard against unwanted inquiry or change. More likely, it is merely a result of the fragmentary and disorganized character of the system; but the effect is the same as if the system wished to protect itself from scrutiny.

THE MISMATCH OF SERVICES AND CLIENTS

There has been, since the turn of the century, a significant change in the makeup of those people identified as blind. In the period between 1900 and the 1930's, the blind were identified primarily as children and adults of working age. The dominant causes of blindness were war, industrial accident, and disease, and the blind were likely to have only the single handicap of blindness. During the 1930's, federal and state aid to the blind came into being on a significant scale, carried along on the wave of New Deal social legislation. This period of change saw the establishment of certain major programs for the blind. *The sheltered workshop,* publicly or privately supported, trained blind adults for occupations thought to be particularly appropriate to the blind—piano tuner, for example, or broom maker, or vending stand operator. *The school for the blind* provided separate track, physically segregated education for the blind child. And in the early 1940's, state *vocational legislation* promoted rehabilitation for adults of working age. All such programs treated fitness for work and economic independence through employment as the central tests of rehabilitation.

Today, the makeup of the blind has changed. The population of the severely visually impaired in the United States is now heavily weighted toward (1) the aged blind (2) the multiple-handicapped, especially among children (3) the poor ethnic minorities, especially the low skilled (4) those with significant residual vision. All sources indicate that a high percentage of the blind are persons over 65, although the estimates vary from 40 percent (MRA) to 65 percent (NHS, which uses a broader, functional definition of blindness). The dominant causes of blindness today are senile degeneration, diabetes, and other multiple etiologies characteristic of old age and, among children, genetic and prenatal influences which tend to be associated with other disabilities in addition to blindness. The overall pattern, both for the aged and for children, is one of multiple disability. Projections of the prevalence of blindness and the makeup of the blind to 1970 and 1985 suggest that, with the increase in the numbers of persons over 65, these trends will continue.

These developments mean that, for an increasing majority of the blind, economic employment is an unrealistic goal. *Nevertheless, agencies for the blind continue to behave as though this shift in the blind population had not taken place.* In the selection of clients and the provision of services, their programs are oriented to work or to education leading to work. They measure the success of their services in terms of their clients' achievement of some measure of economic independence. Only a small number of significant exceptions to this general pattern exist within the blindness system.

At the time of its inception, each of these work-oriented programs represented a significant innovation in what was considered humane treatment for the blind. Yet each has tended to become established and frozen in place as an aspect of the way services to the blind "must" operate. Thus, the blindness system today is an array of agencies and services dating from different periods, based on different assumptions concerning the character of the blind population, pursuing different goals, and using different technologies. The effect is rather like complex geological strata in which substances of widely varying origins and characters exist side by side.

The result is that the official blindness system provides services to only a relatively small fraction of those who are actually blind and eligible for assistance. Since the services offered are largely education, rehabilitation, and care, *only about 20 percent of the total blind population are actually being served today.* In general, these 20 percent are either children with the single handicap of blindness or adults of working age and potential for employment. The 80 percent who receive no services tend to be those without apparent potential for employment or educational advancement: the aged, the multiple handicapped, the poor, and the low skilled. Such persons are shunted off to other systems which provide minimal income-maintenance or custodial care, or are ignored. A substantial portion of the 80 percent may receive some form of support from the informal system of family, friends, and community.[5]

Why have the design and mix of official services been so unresponsive to changes in the needs and capacities of the blind? The answer is that, for good bureaucratic reasons, agencies tend to behave as if they believed that the blind need, or should have, *the services which happen to be offered by the agencies* rather than that agencies should modify services in response to changing characteristics of the blind population. This is true both of the kinds of services offered and of the methods or techniques by which such services are delivered. To be sure, there are exceptions. But in the case of services designed specifically for the "newer" categories of the blind, the exceptions do not exceed three agencies in each category. And even in the case of services designed for more traditional categories of the blind—mobility training, comprehensive rehabilitation, or training in the use of low vision aids—only a few agencies have shown themselves to be innovative in any significant degree. Taken together, these exceptional, change-oriented agencies constitute only a tiny fraction of the entire official blindness system. The overwhelming pattern remains firmly based on the assumption that "the blind" are employable adults, children with the single handicap of blindness,

5. See the study conducted by the Bureau of Labor Statistics for the American Foundation for the Blind, "National Survey of Personnel Standards and Personnel Practices and Services for the Blind—1955."

and the totally blind. The shifting population of the blind has falsified that assumption, yet the pattern of programs remains.

STRATEGIES, CONSTRAINTS

Why does this blindness system behave in such a fashion? One important factor is to be found in the purposes of the organizations and individuals who serve the blind. Now, because the system is in reality a *non*system, there is no group or institution capable of setting a common objective for all elements of the blindness system. Nevertheless, it is clear from the statements of participants and observers that there are three main objectives which enjoy widespread currency, in practice or in rhetoric, within the blindness system:

1. Minimize the cost to the blindness system of providing services to the blind. This is the principle of "least cost to the system itself."
2. Minimize the cost to the nation of providing services.
3. Optimize human functioning for the blind. This objective, frequently voiced by professionals within the system, focuses on what services may enable the blind to *do* or *become,* rather than the economic criteria of performance.

Each of these objectives implies a different strategy for allocating resources and defining configurations of service and coverage.

Least cost to the blindness system. If it were to operate under this principle alone, the blindness system would provide services only to those blind people who are likely to be able to enter the labor force. This way, the system encounters only those who can be trained to leave the blindness system quickly, thereby maximizing turnover rates and minimizing the cost to the blindness system. Hence, the system would select children with the single handicap of blindness and adults of working age and would provide them with education and instrumental and vocational services. The others—multiple-handicapped children, adults over 44, etc.—it would either shunt off to other systems or provide with minimal care or maintenance.

Least cost to the nation. Under this principle, the system would operate much as it does under the first principle. The main difference is that, under this second objective, it would be far less selective in providing educational, instrumental, or vocation services. The cumulative costs of income maintenance or custodial care are so great that it is cost-effective to give job-oriented services to all individuals for whom there is *any* finite chance that they will be able to leave the system. The first objective, which does not require the blindness system to bear the costs of long-term maintenance or support of those blind who are unable to work, provides the system with no incentive to behave this way.

Here, the analysis touches on a peculiar and interesting feature of the blindness system. *Those who must decide whether or not to provide services to an individual are institutionally separated from those who stand the cost and trouble of long-term maintenance and care.* The current system's fragmentation removes the incentive to provide services so as to avoid later maintenance and care.

Optimize human functioning. This objective implies that, even if there is no possibility of his gaining economic independence, it is worth devoting resources to a blind person in order to make him function somewhat more independently. This means, in other words, that an additional benefit—personal independence—counts in offsetting costs incurred in the system. The consequence of such an objective, of course, is to increase the cost of operating the system. In 1966, for example, an additional $1 billion (on a base of about $446 million) would have been needed for a blindness system which attempted to maximize human functioning. A very large portion of that increase would have gone for services to the aged.[6]

In terms of these three models, the current blindness system is a hybrid. With respect to the way in which it determines what categories of the blind shall receive services, it functions according to the principle of the least cost to the system itself. Those blind without high potential for gainful employment are either ignored or shunted off to other systems (such as welfare, veterans' care, etc.). But with respect to those whom it *does* select for training or care, the blindness system tends to behave as if its purpose were to optimize their human functioning. Its expenditures on the blind it chooses to encounter are high.

THE AGENCY AS A HOMEOSTATIC SYSTEM

It is remarkable that the network of blindness agencies has been able to keep its traditional modes of operation intact. That it has done so is not the result of any conscious or systematic policy. Rather, little change has occurred because the structure of the system itself affects the way in which individual agencies set their goals and allocate their resources.

The blindness system is horizontally and vertically fragmented. Public and private agencies tend to be cut off from one another, and even the major public

6. Although the money costs of this third system are important, the problem of manpower resources constitutes an even more powerful constraint. It is estimated that the official blindness system employs approximately 10,000 today. *For a blindness system designed to optimize the human functioning of the entire blind population of the U.S., approximately 118,000 employees would be needed.* (The bulk of them would be engaged in providing services to those over the age of 44.) Even under the principle of "least cost to the system itself," *68,000* employees would be necessary if the system were to encounter all of the blind.

These estimates are based on the assumption that all blind people would be covered, that programs would be designed to meet the special disabilities and potentials of different categories of the blind, and that there would be no change in current methods and technologies. *Clearly, it will be impossible to assure universal coverage of the blind until radical improvements are made in the character of services, the structure of jobs and manpower in relation to services, or in the technology of services to the blind.*

agencies function separately. There is discontinuity among national, state, and local levels. Public laws, jurisdictional rules, agency policies, and provisions governing the use of private dollars—all these tend to lock service units into artificial boundaries and prevent the system from modifying its behavior in face of changing client demand. Moreover, the system's isolation from other service systems—health or welfare, for example—makes it difficult to cut across system boundaries in order to insure that all the blind will have a full range of comprehensive services. And finally, the blindness system consists of only a few large agencies and many small ones. Most of these latter are dependent on grass roots support, particularly in the form of private endowment, and are therefore capable of resisting public pressure for change. The result is that there exist almost no points at which public action might effectively move the system as a whole.

In the context of such fragmentation, the discretion of individual agencies is used in a way that works against change. Consider these major elements of agency discretion:

Control of client access. Agencies can limit their services to "good" clients and can actually seek out clients meeting their criteria. In large cities, for example, there is active competition for children who are blind only. And the parents of such children often learn to go "agency shopping" as a result.

Control of the duration of the client's stay. Agencies are often free to determine how long they will serve a client. Agencies tend to keep "good" clients for longer periods of time than "bad" clients—months instead of weeks, and not infrequently for years.

Control of the portion of the client's "life space" which the agency takes up. Agencies may, at their discretion, extend their services not only to disabilities directly relevant to blindness, such as those associated with reading or travel, but to the client's overall health, his family relations, his psychological well-being, and the like. At one extreme, the agency becomes the client's total environment.

Control of investment per client. As scope of service and duration of stay increase, the agency increases its dollar and manpower investment in individual clients.

Through the manipulation of these discretionary "values," agencies tend to behave like homeostatic systems. *They can and do compensate for a declining population of the "right" sorts of clients by increasing their investment in the clients they do serve*—all under the justification of improving the quality of service. As a consequence, the agency staff remains stable even though client populations decrease. The agency behaves as though it were optimizing the use of its existing resources.

This homeostatic system is self-reinforcing, but it also depends on a number of factors which are both incentives to and means by which agencies maintain something like a stable state. There is, for example, an ideology still in good currency among professionals within the blindness system. It centers on concern with individuals rather than with numbers, on high standards of service as defined by the profession, on "worthy" clients, and on professionalism conceived as a definition of roles both for the provider and for the user of service. This ideology encourages the agencies' homeostatic tendencies: after all, if worthy clients deserve the highest quality professional service, then one need not be overly concerned with the numerous, invisible others.

Another factor reinforcing the tendency toward homeostasis is the chaotic nature of information about the blindness system. Associated with this is the systematic failure of most agencies to pursue follow-up studies. They simply do not make a practice of discovering what happens to their clients after service is completed and clients are discharged from agency care. As a result, the entire system is deprived of, and protected from, the opportunity to learn from its successes and failures.

THE SOURCES OF INNOVATION

During the past 25 or 30 years, there have been a few significant innovations in serving the blind. Because new technologies and methods must play a large role in any improvement in service to the blind, it seems worthwhile to consider two of the more interesting cases of innovation.

The only important technical innovation in travel for the blind in this century has been the "long cane" method, which is the invention of Dr. Richard Hoover. It consists in replacing the old orthopedic cane with a light, long cane, the purpose of which is to sense the environment rather than to serve as a support. The long cane precedes the training foot in an oscillating motion and permits the skillful user to move rather rapidly over varied terrain. Hoover, a former physical education instructor, developed the cane while serving in a U.S. Army group set up to provide rehabilitation for blinded World War II veterans. At the time, accepted practice in the blindness system was to assume that the blind have little capability for travel and that what little such capability could be developed required instruction from a teacher who was himself blind. (This approach is still in currency in many sectors of the blindness system.) The group of blind veterans were for the most part vigorous and healthy. They found that little or no rehabilitation had been prepared for them, and they besieged the commanding general, pounding with their canes on his desk, demanding the program they had been promised. It was in this context that Hoover was given an opportunity to develop and teach his method. That method was revolutionary in its assumptions that the blind could travel independently, that a long antennalike cane could help them, and that a sighted instructor could teach them.

The introduction of the long cane technique was an unusual event which was quite out of keeping with the traditional behavior of the blindness system. Seen against the backdrop of such traditional behavior, three special circumstances characterize its introduction. First, the champion of the invention was an "outsider." Hoover had previously worked in blindness agencies, but merely as a physical education instructor. It was only later that he became an ophthalmologist. Second, the invention was precipitated by a dislocating, crisislike event for which the system had no prepared response. And third, there was a strong and active group of blind clients who were in a position to make demands and to enforce them.

Consider, as a second case, the entry of blind children into public schools, which dates from the 1950s. Previously, it had been assumed that blind children could be educated only in a separate school which provided them with the security of being together and which catered exclusively to their special needs. The story of the opening of public schools to blind children is connected to a disease called retrolentil-fibroplasin, which affects premature infants and which was discovered in the 1950s, (a story in itself) to be a consequence of excessive oxygen delivered to the infants in their incubators. Premature infants reared in incubators tended to be children of middle-class parents. The movement to introduce blind children into the public schools and to provide a program of supplementary aids in reading and communications skills began among groups of middle-class mothers, initially in California, who found the physically segregated education offered their children repellent and who organized to develop an alternative to it.

Again, there were two special features of this innovation in services to the blind. First, there existed a crisis situation created by a demand the system was not prepared to handle. The number of retrolentils grew precipitously in the 1950s and declined soon after the cause of the disease was discovered. And second, there was a strong and active group of service-users, in this case relatively well-to-do, who organized to enforce their demands.

It should not be supposed that innovations are an untarnished good. Characteristically, innovations which at the time represent humane advances—the vocational rehabilitation movement of the 1940s comes to mind—survive to inhibit the system's response to the *next* requirement and thus become a part of its dynamic conservatism. Any new innovation achieves success and acceptance only through a kind of warfare on the old.

A STRATEGY FOR CHANGE

Several requirements for change have so far emerged. First, the blindness system should reallocate its priorities so that it makes a firm commitment to encounter every blind person. Second, the system should reallocate its priorities toward subcategories of the blind so that the design of its services reflects changes in the makeup of the blind population. Third, the organization and technology of services must be restructured so that services are appropriate to the needs of the great majority of the blind and so that current manpower constraints can be circumvented. Fourth, the social systems and supporting ideologies of the blindness agencies must be made compatible with the restructured priorities and services. Finally, the methods of data gathering and processing must be changed so that the blindness system can become an effective learning system.

Some of the specific kinds of change flowing from these requirements are as follows:

Diffusion of best practice. One of the characteristic features of the blindness system is the large gap between agency practice considered "best" by experts inside and outside the field, and the practice of the majority of agencies. This is true even of a new technique like the long cane, which has made surprisingly little progress in penetrating the blindness system since its introduction in the 1940s. The same is true of training in low vision aids, comprehensive rehabilitation and the public school track for education of blind children. In the case of services for multiple-handicapped children and the aged the gap is so great that best practice is virtually the *only* practice. In the language of business, there has been very little market penetration, and the reasons for this lie largely in the fragmentation of the blindness system.

It has become clear that the mere existence of pilot projects does not of itself insure widespread adoption of new practice even if that practice is of established effectiveness. The dynamic conservatism of the system means that an active strategy of change is required—one that creates pressures and incentives for the building of new capacity at the same time that it creates demand for that capacity. Demonstrations, information-dissemination, and training are necessary but not sufficient conditions for the diffusion of best practice.

New models of integrated service. There exists a pressing need for integration of services to the blind. On one level, services related specifically to blindness (training in reading or mobility, for example) must be integrated with services relating to health, employment, or financial support so that a blind person need not negotiate several totally disconnected systems. On a second level, services relating to the improvement or use of residual vision must be integrated with services relating to blindness. Low-vision aid clinics, generally limited in their scope to aid in reading, tend to be disconnected from the bulk of services to the blind, which proceed as if the client had no vision at all. And finally, there is a need for *reintegrating* services around *new* characteristics of the blind person. Given the increasing incidence of the aged blind and the rising rate of multiple-handicapped in that group, it is relevant to ask if services to the aged might more effectively be organized around age rather than around blindness.

All such forms of integration would require the establishment and management of networks of service—that is, of linked arrays of agencies. There would be far greater emphasis than at present on infrastructure functions like admissions, screening, diagnosis, referral, "tracking" individuals through the system, guidance, and evaluation. Network management would emerge as the central form of leadership within the system.

Power in the hands of users. If the idea of integration points in the direction of a greater connectedness in the blindness system, then the notion of vesting power over service in the client points in the direction of a special kind of decentralization. Such a change would affect not only the manner in which services are delivered but the process through which services change over time, both of which would become rather like a market mechanism. At least three variants on this theme suggest themselves:

1. Establishment of "contract managers." These agents would be separately funded to provide services to given populations of the blind but would not manage service-providing bureaucracies. Instead, they would contract with other agencies, old and new, to provide services on request. Contract managers would have the freedom to shift contracts on the basis of observed performance. The intent would be to free managers from the job of maintaining their own bureaucracies and hence from the pressures to optimize the use of their own staffs.
2. Establishments of ombudsmen for the blind. Their function would be to help blind persons negotiate the service system. Independently funded, they would represent the interests of the blind in dealing with the agencies.
3. Direct payments to the blind. The blind could be given funds with which to purchase services, either from established agencies or from new ones that might come into being to serve a new market.

None of these changes will emerge from a single approach which relies for its effect on the manipulation of one factor alone, such as manpower, funding patterns, or ideology. The dynamic conservatism of the blindness system has multiple roots which will yield only to multiple attack. Such a multiple attack must be of a "critical mass" appropriate to overcoming the system's conservatism. It must embrace a number of programs which are mutually consistent or at least not mutually inhibiting. It must address itself to the few leverage points in the blindness system. And perhaps most important of all, an effective multiple approach must insure that the blindness system will become an effective learning system. The system will not learn what to do unless it becomes more capable of learning; it will not act on the basis of its learning unless it is made to do so by forces which are commensurate with its own resistance to change.

Small–Site Industrial Renewal Program

INTRODUCTION

This report[1] contains analysis of a proposed program to use the city's urban renewal powers to assemble small industrial sites. These sites would be sold (at "write-down" prices) to firms or developers. The target firms would consist of those firms which otherwise would migrate from the city primarily because of the lack of suitable space for expansion. The city would also undertake to train new workers hired by the firms moving to the sites.

Need

1. The city has large numbers of unemployed, sub-employed, and welfare recipients—the target group.
2. Paradoxically, there is a shortage of jobs suitable to the existing skill-levels of many members of the target group, but jobs are available which demand skills greater than those now possessed by most of the target group.
3. Despite a 6 percent rise in total city employment in the ten years between 1958 and 1967, jobs in the manufacturing sector fell by 11 percent—a loss of 100,000 jobs. Jobs are expanding in New York, but not in the manufacturing sector which is the most likely source of employment for members of our target group.
4. A significant factor in the continuing decline of manufacturing in New York City is the out-migration of firms seeking space for expansion. In 1965, for example, 153 plants migrated; the city consequently lost 12,000 jobs. However, 91 percent relocated in nearby New York or New Jersey counties, indicating their preference for the New York City area.

Findings

1. The proposed program represents only a small part of the ultimate solution to the problem of welfare and unemployment.
2. It is, however, a practical and immediate step in the right direction.

---

1. This example was prepared by Graeme M. Taylor based on original work done by Jack Toby of the Budget Bureau, city of New York.

3. The city presently contains suitable space in sufficient quantities for the program to make an impact.
4. In rough, order-of-magnitude terms, the proposed program has a benefit-cost ratio of 2:1, considering only dollar benefits to the city.
5. A net investment by the city of $9 million annually (loss on sale of land plus training) would provide small sites totaling 100 acres. This would result in:[2]
   a) creation of 1,400 new jobs
   b) preventing 1,200 familites from becoming welfare recipients
   c) removal of 350 families from welfare
   d) saving the city $18 million, in present value terms, in welfare payments and taxes

The above statements and findings are documented in the following report and in the three appendices: I, Economic Analysis; II, Unemployment and Welfare in New York City; and III, Decline of Manufacturing in New York City.

ANALYSIS

From Table 11 in Appendix III, we see that the average space occupied by migrant plants in their new locations outside New York City was approximately 41,000 square feet. Appendix III indicates that, for approximately 75 percent of 153 firms migrating from New York City in 1965, space problems were a factor in their decision to leave the city. Very roughly, then, we can infer that these firms *might* have remained in New York City if a total of 6.4 million square feet of industrial space had been available (*a*) at a reasonable cost, and (*b*) with elimination of the problems of site assembly faced by a private firm.

$$75\% \times 153 \times 41,000 \times 1.33 = 6.4 \text{ million square feet}$$
(where 1.33:1 is the assumed average ratio of floor
space to land area)

Thus, in order to have retained 115 firms and 9,200 jobs lost to the city in 1965 due to space problems, 115 plots of land averaging roughly 1 1/4 acres would have been required. (*Note:* 1 acre = 43,560 square feet)

The remainder of this analysis consists of three sections which deal in turn with the following questions:
1. Space inventory: Does sufficient suitable space exist?
2. Proposed program: How would the proposed program operate?
3. Economic analysis: What are the dollar costs and benefits to the city of the proposed program.

2. These figures are based on certain critical assumptions detailed in Table 6.

Space Inventory

Procedure
1. November 1966 aerial photographs were examined to locate areas of vacant and underutilized land.
2. Most of these areas were inspected in person in August, 1967. Areas obviously going residential were eliminated and some new areas added.
3. Areas were checked with Sanborn land use maps and zoning maps. Areas surrounded by residential uses or zoned residential were eliminated unless a good reason existed for retaining them (such as a vacant plot adjacent to an incinerator in a residentially zoned area).

Estimates
Estimates of available space in the area are shown in Table 1.

Table 1
Estimates of Available Space

Bronx (1)	7,200,000 square feet	165 acres
Brooklyn (2)	7,000,000 square feet	161 acres
Manhattan	350,000 square feet	8 acres
Queens (3)	10,150,000 square feet	233 acres
Total (4)	24,700,000 square feet	567 acres

1. Additional space of approximately 2,000,000 square feet or 46 acres appears to be available in railroad land not being used for trackage or buildings in the South Bronx.
2. Additional space of approximately 3,000,000 square feet or 69 acres is occupied by the Brooklyn Union Gas Company on Newtown Creek and is only lightly covered. However, this appears to be an active installation.
3. Additional space of 11,000,000 square feet or 250 acres is occupied by a primarily coal-burning Consolidated Edison operation on Berian's Island, a peninsula in the northwest corner of Queens. The westerly part of this parcel is tentatively slated for a park.
4. These figures do not include land, a substantial portion of which is in warehouse or in-use industrial use. An inspection would probably turn up substantial amounts of land in this category which is also underutilized. However, the figures above are probably fairly close to the amount of land in plots of an acre or more which could be redeveloped industrially with little or no relocation.

Proposed Program

It is proposed that the city use urban renewal powers contained in Article XV of the General Municipal Law to acquire and transfer to a firm or developer suitable parcels of land for industrial redevelopment. Preference would be given to firms which (1) would otherwise leave the city (2) are expanding their work force (3) are willing to operate or participate in a training program.

The program would operate as shown in the simplified flow chart, Table 2.

Table 2
Simplified Flow Chart of Proposed Industrial Renewal Program

Time			
			Urban renewal process

Site identification and acquisition	- City surveys
	- Suggestions
	  from firms
	- Offerings
		- Selection of
		  sites or areas
			- (Acquisition and disposition of land to firm or developer)

Obtaining firms	- Inquiries from
	  firms
	- Response to
	  publicity
	- Early warning
	  system
		- Selection of
		  firms
			- Negotiations

Training			- Establish manpower training as required

The city would identify potential sites, either in advance or in response to a firm's request, offerings from landowners, or suggestions from interested firms. Simultaneously, the city would learn of candidate firms through inquiries, possibly in response to publicity regarding the program, or from the existing "early warning system" under which banks and other organizations alert the city about impending business migrations. Sites and firms would be matched; the urban renewal process would be set in motion to acquire the land; the site would be prepared and any necessary relocations accomplished; negotiations with the firm would be concluded and manpower training programs established as needed.

Economic Analysis

In order to evaluate the economics of the proposed program, we shall examine the costs and benefits *to New York City* of averting the migration from the city of one plant.

We shall make the following *assumptions:*

1. A one-story factory is constructed on the new lot.
2. All the employees in the old NYC plant move with the company to the new NYC plant.
3. The cost of city services does not increase.
4. The new lot is vacant; hence, demolition and relocation costs are zero and the assessed value of the property increases only by the assessed value of the new building constructed on the site.
5. The firm expands on moving, both in terms of total square feet and total employment.
6. Some of the new employees will require training by the city.
7. Had the company migrated from NYC, some employees would have moved with the firm; some would have remained behind and been unable to find new employment.

The relevant *costs* to the city are as follows:

1. Capital costs—acquiring the land, demolition, relocation of existing occupants (if necessary), and project administration.
2. Training costs—training new workers hired by the company when it moves to the new location.

The relevant *dollar benefits* to the city are as follows:

1. Receipts from sale of land to the firm or developer.
2. Net real estate tax gain to the city through tax revenues assessed on the new building constructed at the new location.
3. Savings in welfare payments when the company expands its work force drawing on those currently receiving welfare payments from the city.
4. Savings in welfare payments through avoidance of new welfare recipients being added to the rolls (this would occur if the company migrated leaving behind a number of employees who are unable to find new employment).
5. Retention of revenues from corporate taxes (other than real estate) that would have been lost to the city had the company moved.
6. Retention of revenues from taxes paid by employees that would have been lost to the city had the company moved.

The sample calculations worked out in Appendix I revealed further results concerning benefits, costs, and cumulative net benefits, as shown in Table 4.

Appendix I presents a detailed economic analysis of the dollar costs and benefits to New York City of averting migration of one plant. In Table 3, the results are summarized for a plant assumed to require 30,000 square feet of building space in its new location.

Table 3
Costs and Benefits of Averting Migration of One Plant

Costs	Estimate
1. Site acquisition, demolition, and relocation	$200,000
2. Training costs	10,000
Total city costs:	$210,000
Benefits	*Estimate*
1. Revenues from sale of land	$120,000
2. Real estate tax gain	150,000[a]
3. Welfare payments saved (removed from current rolls)	34,000[b]
4. Welfare payments saved (avoid generating new recipients)	52,000[c]
5. Retention of corporate city taxes	53,000[d]
6. Retention of personal city taxes	4,000[e]
Total dollar benefits to city: $413,000	

a. The figure of $150,000 for the real estate tax gain represents the present value of a gain of $12,600 per year for 20 years discounted at 6 percent.

b. The figure of $34,000 for welfare payments saved (removal from current rolls) represents the present value of a saving of $4,500 per year for 10 years discounted at 6 percent.

c. The figure of $52,000 for welfare payments saved (avoid generating new recipients) represents the present value of a saving of $12,000 per year for 5 years discounted at 6 percent.

d. The figure of $53,000 for retention of corporate city taxes represents the present value of a saving of $4,500 per year for 20 years discounted at 6 percent.

e. The figure of $4,000 for retention of personal city taxes represents the present value of a saving of $323 per year for 20 years, discounted at 6 percent.

Table 4
Further Costs, Benefits, and Net Benefits of Averting Migration of One Plant

Benefits	
New jobs created	= 14
Jobs saved	= 12
Families removed from welfare	= 3.5
Land required in new site	= approximately 1 acre
Costs	
Net loss to city as a real estate transaction	= ($80,000)
Training costs (7 trainees @ $1,500)	($10,000)
Total city investment (net)	($90,000)
Cumulative Net Benefits (when present value of following savings included)	
Real estate tax gain ($150,000)	+ $60,000
and Welfare savings ($86,000)	+ $146,000
and Tax savings ($57,000)	+ $203,000

The above calculations can be repeated, of course, using different values for the variables. Every effort was made to use conservative values in the sample calculation. The results probably indicate a rough order of magnitude of the dollar benefits to be expected. If this is so, then we can make the following estimates:

1. The "benefit-cost ratio" of the project analyzed = 2:1
2. For each acre of new site space utilized, the city would gain 14 jobs, remove 3.5 families from the welfare rolls, and prevent 12 families from becoming welfare recipients.

Thus, if the city *annually* assisted 100 firms to relocate within the city, each requiring approximately one acre of site space, we get the results in Table 5.

Table 5
Costs of Relocating 100 Firms within City

City investment required (net)	= $9 million per year
Land required	= 100 acres per year (4,356,000 sq. ft.)
New jobs created	= 1,400 per year
Jobs saved	= 1,200 per year
Families removed from welfare	= 350 per year
Families prevented from becoming welfare recipients	= 1,200 per year

It must be emphasized that the above conclusions are based on a *sample* calculation; many assumptions were made in selecting values for the variables. More refined estimates could be made and substituted in the formulas presented in Appendix I to calculate the costs and benefits for actual proposed projects.

APPENDIX I

ECONOMIC ANALYSIS: Benefits and Costs to New York City of Averting Migration of One Plant

Preliminary Comments on Methodology

The following analysis is performed from the viewpoint of New York City; i.e., costs and benefits will be counted as relevant only in so far as they affect city revenues or disbursements. This approach *ignores:*
1. Opportunity costs
2. Real resource costs
3. Costs and benefits as viewed by the state or federal governments
4. Costs and benefits as perceived by individual citizens

   (1) *Opportunity costs:* An opportunity cost is measured by benefits foregone (sacrificed). In this case, an example of an opportunity cost would be revenues or benefits from a site if used for purposes other than small-site industrial renewal. For example, if the site were used for a high-rise apartment building, presumably real-estate tax revenues would be different from revenues if the site were used for a factory. Or if the site were used for a new school, hospital, or park, benefits to the citizens might be greater (though harder to measure) than benefits from retention of one factory.

   (2) *Real resource costs:* As distinct from money costs, real resource costs attempt to measure the value of resources produced or consumed. From a national point of view, for example, welfare payments are *not* considered real resource costs. Welfare payments are not payments for goods or services produced; they are rather "transfer payments"—money is transferred from the pockets of one group in society (taxpayers) to another group (welfare recipients) with no concomitant increase in national wealth.

   (3) *Federal and state viewpoints:* The analysis would have been performed quite differently if done from the standpoint of the federal or state government. For example, the federal government is primarily concerned with reducing real resource costs and increasing real resource benefits. Ignoring income redistribution effects, the federal government is presumably not interested in promoting a program which keeps a firm in New York City at the expense of, say, Connecticut. From a national standpoint, it is hardly relevant whether there are 100 employed

persons in New York City and 100 welfare recipients in Norwalk, or vice versa. Similarly, from the viewpoint of New York State, it is immaterial whether we raise employment in Buffalo or New York City. For the purposes of a city decision maker, however, the adoption of a "city-centered" approach is, of course, perfectly logical.

(4) *Costs and benefits as perceived by individual citizens:* We have counted as benefits, for example, only city taxes paid by citizens—not their total earnings. To an individual, of course, it is clearly more important to earn a good wage as an employee than to receive a lesser amount in welfare. Also, we have not counted certain differential costs that may be imposed on individuals; for example, if a firm remains in the city but moves to a new site several miles from its original location, employees will presumably incur different transportation costs from before.

Variables Used in the Analysis

Table 6 shows the variables used in the analysis. Many of the variables have been expressed in terms of their relationship to X_N—the number of square feet of new building space occupied by the firm. The rationale for this approach is that industrial space is *the* scarce commodity of primary concern to those who will operate the program. Presumably, therefore, they will be most interested in formulae which will readily permit them to translate space availability into dollars of cost and benefit. The analysis could readily be recast, if desired, in terms of work-force figures or "old" space requirements, for example.

Assumptions

We shall make the following *assumptions:*
1. A one-story factory is constructed on the new lot.
2. All the employees in the old NYC plant move with the company to the new NYC plant.
3. The cost of city services does not increase.
4. The new lot is vacant; hence, demolition and relocation costs are zero and the assessed value of the property increases only by the assessed value of the new building constructed on the site.
5. The firm expands on moving, both in terms of total square feet and total employment.
6. Some of the new employees will require training by the city.
7. Had the company migrated from NYC, some employees would have moved with the firm; some would have remained behind and been unable to find new employment.

Table 6
Variables in Economic Analysis

Values used in sample calculation	Symbol	Variables used in the analysis Explanation
1.3	I	Increase in plant floor area from old location to new location, based on sample of firms moving from NYC to new plants within and outside NYC.
23,078	X_o	Sq. ft. of old building space occupied
30,000	X_N	Sq. ft. of new building space occupied, $X_N = (I)(X_o)$
0.75	B	Floor/area ratio or ratio of plant floor space to land. The maximum floor/area ratio for the lightest manufacturing zoning is i.0; we assume a 1-story plant on 75% of the land, leaving space for parking, sidewalks, etc.
$4.50	C_A	Cost per square foot of land acquisition, based on 1967 cost of 90–100% vacant industrial land in Bronx, Brooklyn, Queens
$0	C_D	Cost per square foot of demolition
$0	C_R	Cost per square foot of relocation
$0.50	C_C	Cost per square foot of administration of industrial renewal program. Arbitrary.
$1,500	C_t	Cost to the city of training one new, inexperienced semi- "hard-core" employee. The average training cost for a full year program was about $3,000 in 1967, and this assumes a six-month training period.
50%	t	% of additional workers who must be trained. Arbitrary; this is a *goal* for bringing hard-core workers into better-paying industrial jobs.
500	S	Sq. ft. of building space per worker in new building. This is approximately the average space requirement for newer plants in NYC.
$3	R	Resale revenue per sq. ft. of land. This is lower than what we would expect to get, but we wanted to work in a writedown and see how feasible the program would be. The writedown assumed here is 40%.

Table 6 (cont'd)

Values used in sample calculation	Symbol	Variables used in the analysis Explanation
10%	N_L	% of old work force which would have moved with firm if it had moved outside NYC. Arbitrary.
$70	T_L	City sales and income taxes paid per year by one worker. Approximately what a worker earning $6,000 per year would pay.
20	Y	Probable life of city's investment, in years. Approximately the normal life of bonds issued by city for urban renewal projects.
20%	N_u	% of old work force who would have remained unemployed if plant had left city. Arbitrary.
5	Y_o	Number of years the N_u would have been on welfare. Arbitrary.
$1,300	W	Annual city cost for welfare payments to family of unemployed worker on relief rolls. City's share is about 33%, depending on program.
25%	N_w	% of additional workers who come from welfare rolls. Arbitrary.
10	Y_N	Years the N_w workers would have remained on welfare. Arbitrary.
$12	C	Construction cost per square foot. Approximately 1967 construction cost for single story industrial space in NYC.
70%	V	Equalization rate, or percent of value assessed for real estate tax purposes. NYC's equalization rate is between 60% and 70%, depending on the year and borough.
5%	r	Property tax rate, approximately NYC's 1967 rate.
$0.15	T	Other than property taxes paid by company per square foot of building space. Arbitrary; includes water charges, sales taxes on purchases over old-location levels, etc.

Costs

The relevant *costs* to the city are as follows:

1. Capital costs—acquiring the land, demolition, relocation of existing occupants (if necessary), and project administration.
2. Training costs—training new workers hired by the company when it moves to the new location.

Benefits

The relevant *dollar benefits* to the city are as follows:

1. Receipts from sale of land to the firm or developer.
2. Net real estate tax gain to the city through tax revenues assessed on the new building constructed at the new location.
3. Savings in welfare payments when the company expands its work force drawing on those currently receiving welfare payments from the city.
4. Savings in welfare payments through avoidance of new welfare recipients being added to the rolls (this would occur if the company migrated leaving behind a number of employees who are unable to find new employment).
5. Retention of revenues from corporate taxes (other than real estate) that would have been lost to the city had the company moved.
6. Retention of revenues from taxes paid by employees that would have been lost to the city had the company moved.

Using the variables identified in Table 6, we can establish the following components of cost and benefit to New York City.

Investment Required by New York City

1. *Capital costs:* The cost of site acquisition, demolition, and relocation, plus project administration costs. For a new site whose land area is

$$\frac{X_N}{B}, \text{ this equals } \frac{X_N}{B}(C_A + C_D + C_R + C_C).$$

Note: project administration costs will have a "fixed" and a "variable" component. The fixed component will contain such items as departmental overhead, i.e., items which do not vary with the number of projects undertaken. The variable component will depend on, for example, the size and complexity of the project. However, for purposes of simplifying the calculations, it is assumed that project administration costs are entirely variable, and are proportional to the area of the site. Since project administration costs are a very small component of total costs, this simplifying assumption will not seriously imperil the validity of our model.

2. *Training costs:* The training costs are simply the number of workers who must be trained multiplied by the average cost to the city of training one worker for the new plant.

Square feet of floor space in old building = X_N divided by I (the "factor of increase, "i.e., the ratio of new space to old space)

$$\text{Number of employees in old building} = \frac{X_N}{IS}$$

$$\text{Number of employees in new building} = \frac{X_N}{S}$$

Thus, increased number of employees expressed in terms of floor space =

$$\frac{X_N}{S} - \frac{X_N}{IS}$$

Not all these new workers will require training by the city. If t is the percent of new workers who do require training, and if C_t is the average cost to the city of providing training, then the total training cost to the city is:

$$C_t \cdot t \left(\frac{X_N}{S} - \frac{X_N}{IS} \right) = \frac{C_t \cdot t \cdot X_N}{S} \left(1 - \frac{1}{I} \right)$$

Benefits to New York City

1. The city will obtain revenues from sale of land to the firm or developer. The land area = X_N/B, where B is the ratio of floor space to land area. If R is the sale price of land in dollars per square foot, then city revenues from sale of land = $X_N \cdot R/B$.

2. The next most obvious benefit to the city treasury arises from the increase in real estate tax revenues resulting from construction of a new building on the site. (It is assumed that the new site was vacant; and, therefore, the relevant incremental benefits equal the total tax revenues from the new building.) If X_N = floor space of the new building, C = construction cost per square foot, V = percent assessed valuation, r = percent annual tax rate, and Y *years* = relevant "life" of the building, then the "lifetime" benefits to NYC = Present value of a stream of payments of $(X_N \cdot C \cdot V \cdot r)$ discounted at $P\%$ for Y *years* (where P% is the chosen discount rate).

3. A third benefit will accrue to the city treasury in the form of city welfare

payments saved when the firm hires new employees who are presently welfare recipients. We saw above that the number of new employees was

$$\frac{X_N}{S} \left(1 - \frac{1}{I} \right)$$

If N_W represents the percent of these new employees who are currently recipients of welfare, and if W equals the average annual city cost of providing welfare presently generated by each of these people, and if Y_N is the number of years they would otherwise have remained on welfare, then the savings to the city are: present value of a stream of payments of

$$\frac{N_W \cdot X_N \cdot W}{S} \left(1 - \frac{1}{I} \right)$$

discounted at P% for Y_N years.

4. We must also recognize that, if the firm *had* moved out of New York City, some key employees would have moved with the firm, some would have remained behind and successfully found new employment, but some would have been left behind unable to find new employment. It is likely that the latter would have become welfare recipients. If N_u is the percent of the old work force that would have become welfare recipients, and Y_o the number of years they would remain on welfare, then, using W as the average welfare cost, the relevant savings to the city are: present value of a stream of payments of

$$\frac{N_u \cdot X_N \cdot W}{SI}$$

discounted at $P\%$ for Y_o *years.* (Note: the number of employees in the old location is given by X_N/SI.)

5. The city treasury will also benefit in that it will retain city taxes paid by the firm (other than real estate taxes) which would have been lost if the firm had moved out of the city. If T represents city taxes paid by the firm, expressed in terms of dollars per square foot of new space occupied, then the savings are: Present value of a stream of payments of $(T \cdot X_N)$ discounted at $P\%$ for Y *years*, where Y has the same sense as in (2) above.

6. The final dollar benefit to be considered arises from the fact that the city will retain personal taxes paid by employees of the firm who otherwise would have moved out of the city with the firm. If N_L is the percent of the old work force that would have moved, and if T_L is average annual city taxes paid by each employee, then the relevant savings are: present value of stream of payments of

$$\frac{N_L \cdot X_N \cdot T_L}{SI}$$

discounted at *P%* for *Y years,* where Y has the same sense as in (2) and (5) above, and where the number of employees in the old location is again expressed as X_N/SI.

Cost and Benefit Summary

In summary, then, we have the following general expressions for dollar costs and benefits to the city of averting the migration of one firm:

Costs
1. Capital costs:

$$\frac{X_N}{B} \left(C_A + C_D + C_R + C_C \right)$$

2. Training costs:

$$\frac{C_t \cdot t \cdot X_N}{S} \left(1 - \frac{1}{I} \right)$$

Benefits
1. Offset from sale of land to firm or developer: $X_N \cdot R/B$.
2. Real estate tax gain: Present value of $(X_N \cdot C \cdot V \cdot r)$ for *Y years* @ *P%*.
3. Savings in welfare payments by company hiring new employees from welfare rolls: present value of

$$\frac{N_W \cdot X_N \cdot W}{S} \left(1 - \frac{1}{I} \right) \text{ for } Y_N \text{ years @ } P\%.$$

4. Savings in welfare payments by company staying in city: present value of

$$\frac{N_u \cdot X_N \cdot W}{SI} \quad \text{for } Y_o \text{ years @ } P\%.$$

5. Savings in corporate taxes: present value of $(T \cdot X_N)$ for *Y years* @ *P%*.
6. Savings in personal taxes: present value of $(N_L \cdot X_N \cdot T_L/SI)$ for *Y years* @ *P%*.

Sample Calculation

The following calculation is presented for illustrative purposes, using the rough values for the variables listed in the left-hand column of Table 6.

Costs
1. Capital costs:

$$\frac{(30,000)(\$5)}{.75} = \underline{\$200,000}$$

2. Training costs:

$$\frac{(\$1,500)(50\%)(30,000)}{500}\left(1 - \frac{1}{1.3}\right)= \underline{\$10,000}$$

Benefits
1. Sale of land:

$$\frac{(30,000)(\$3)}{.75} = \underline{\$120,000}$$

2. Real estate tax gain: present value of

$$(30,000)(\$12)(70\%)(5\%) \text{ for 20 years @ 6\%} = \underline{\$150,000}$$

3. Welfare payments saved (removed from current rolls): present value of

$$\frac{(25\%)(30,000)(\$1,300)}{500}\left(1 - \frac{1}{1.3}\right) \text{ for 10 years @ 6\%} = \underline{\$34,000}$$

4. Welfare payments saved (avoid generating new recipients): present value of

$$\frac{(20\%)(30,000)(\$1,300)}{(500)(1.3)} \text{ for 5 years @ 6\%} = \underline{\$52,000}$$

5. Savings in other corporate taxes: present value of:

$$(\$0.15)(30,000) \text{ for 20 years @ 6\%} = \underline{\$53,000}$$

6. Savings in personal taxes: present value of:

$$\frac{(10\%)(30,000)(\$70)}{(500)(1.3)} \text{ for 20 years @ 6\%} = \underline{\$4,000}$$

The sample project thus results in *net* present benefits amounting to:
($120,000) + ($150,000) + ($34,000) + ($52,000) + ($53,000) + ($4,000) − ($200,000) − ($10,000) = $203,000

   The above results are summarized in Table 4. The above calculations can be repeated, of course, using different values for the variables.

Conclusion

Every effort has been made to use conservative values in the preceding sample calculation. The above results probably indicate a rough order of magnitude of the dollar benefits to be expected. If this is so, then we can make the following estimates:

1. The "benefit-cost ratio" of the project analyzed = 2:1

$$\frac{\text{Benefits}}{\text{Costs}} = \frac{\$413,000}{210,000}$$

2. For each acre of new site space utilized, the city would gain 14 jobs, remove 3.5 families from the welfare rolls, and prevent 12 families from becoming welfare recipients.

Thus, if the city *annually* assisted 100 firms to relocate within the city, each requiring approximately one acre of site space, we get the results in Table 5.

APPENDIX II

UNEMPLOYMENT AND WELFARE IN NEW YORK CITY

Unemployment and Sub-Employment

The U.S. Department of Labor published a study "Sub-Employment in the Slums of New York" in November 1966 based on a household survey conducted in cooperation with the New York Department of Labor. The following information is extracted from that report.

The reported November 1966 unemployment rate in the U.S. was 3.7 percent; for the New York metropolitan area as a whole it was 4.0 percent. However, for three New York City areas the figures were higher (see Table 7).

Table 7
Unemployment in New York City

Area	Population	Unemployment Rate, %	Sub-Employment Rate, %
Central Harlem	187,635	8.1	28.6
East Harlem	119,830	9.0	33.1
Bedford-Stuyvesant	219,048	6.2	27.6

The sub-employment index counts as sub-employed:

1. those unemployed in the sense that they are actively looking for work and unable to find it
2. those working only part time when they are trying to get full-time work
3. those heads of households under 65 years who earn less than $60 per week working full time and those individuals under 65 who are not heads of households and earn less than $56 per week in a full-time job
4. half the number of "nonparticipants" in the male 20–64 age group
5. a "conservative and carefully considered estimate" of a male "undercount" group (based on the assumption that the number of males in the area should approximate the number of females as indicated by the general male-female relationship in the population and that half of the unfound males are sub-employed).

The principal reasons for unemployment offered by the unemployed themselves are listed in Table 8.

Table 8
Unemployed Give Reasons for Unemployment

Principal reason identified by unemployed	Central Harlem	East Harlem	Bedford-Stuyvesant
	%	%	%
Lack necessary education and training	43	45	52
Too young or too old	15	23	13
No jobs available	21	8	21
Health problems	7	5	5
Personal problems (e.g., police records)	2	5	3

Table 9 compares distribution of job vacancies in New York with the distribution of jobs last held by the unemployed in the three areas studied:

Table 9
Comparison: Types of Job Vacancies April & November 1966

Occupations	*Job vacancies in New York (April 1966), %*	*Jobs last held by the unemployed in the three areas (November 1966), %*
White collar	43.7	13.6
Craftsmen	12.6	2.8
Operatives	24.1	14.7
Laborers	7.6	21.5
Service	11.9	16.6
Farm	0.1	0
Never worked	--	13.5
Not reported	--	17.3

Welfare

Another study reported the following information.

In January 1968, nearly 25 percent of the jobs in New York City paid $80 per week or less, and 23 percent of the city's population lived in households whose annual income in 1967 was less than $4,000.

In August 1968, 860,000 people under 65 were receiving the newly introduced basic welfare allowances, but it was estimated that this represented only 40 percent of the families with heads under 65 whose incomes fell below the new standards. It was estimated that 1.3 million people would be welfare recipients by June 1970, rising to 1.5 million by June 1973.

Conclusion

In three slum areas studied, the unemployment and sub-employment rates are approximately twice as high and seven times as high, respectively, as the unemployment rate reported for the metropolitan area as a whole. Over 10 percent of the city's population are welfare recipients; another 15 percent are estimated to be eligible for welfare under the new standards.

The number of job vacancies exceed the number of unemployed in all categories except the low-skilled "laborer" and "service" categories. The lack of education and training is most frequently cited as the main reason for being unable to find work, followed by a shortage of available jobs.

Clearly, the need is twofold for those willing and able to work:
1. Provision of jobs suited to existing skill-levels
2. Training the low-skilled to fit them for the jobs that are available.

APPENDIX III

DECLINE OF MANUFACTURING IN NEW YORK CITY

Table 10 and Figure 1 present data on number of persons employed in various sectors in New York City for the years 1958–1967. Employment remained fairly constant in wholesale and retail, finance, transportation, and construction. The "services and miscellaneous" and "government" categories experienced increases of 26 percent and 25 percent respectively. Only the manufacturing category suffered a marked decline—11 percent, representing a loss of approximately 100,000 jobs over the ten-year period.

Table 10

New York City Employment by Sector (1958–1967) in Thousands

Sector	1958	1959	1960	1961	1962	1963	1964	1965	1966	1967
Manufacturing	954	963	947	914	912	879	866	865	871	850
Wholesale & retail	734	740	745	740	739	732	742	749	751	748
Services & miscellaneous	574	590	607	615	629	641	665	681	699	726
Government	405	403	408	415	429	440	448	462	484	506
Finance	374	379	386	396	398	395	394	391	397	409
Transportation	322	321	318	321	313	310	317	318	322	324
Construction	117	123	127	127	139	138	127	111	109	108
Total	3,480	3,519	3,538	3,528	3,559	3,535	3,559	3,577	3,633	3,671

Source: New York State *Employment Review* statistics

Migration of Factories From New York City

In July 1966, Dr. Abraham C. Burstein of the New York City Department of Commerce and Industrial Development published a study titled: "Relocation of

Manufacturing Plants out of New York City in 1965." The following information is derived from that study.

Figure 1
Employment in New York City by Selected Sector

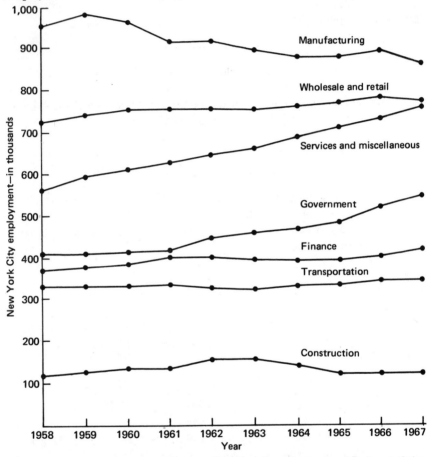

Source: *New York State Employment Review* statistics

A total of 153 manufacturing plants, employing 12,206 workers, moved out of
New York City in 1965.
54 plants, with 4,685 jobs, left Brooklyn
52 plants, with 2,920 jobs, left Manhattan
39 plants, with 3,916 jobs, left Queens
 8 plants, with   685 jobs, left the Bronx.
Of the 153 plants, 139 (91 percent) relocated in nearby New York or New Jersey
counties, 4 in Connecticut, 4 in Pennsylvania, and 6 in more distant states.

The distribution of the migrants, by size of the work force formerly employed in the city, was as follows:

15 employed fewer than 10
20 employed 10 to 19
53 employed 20 to 49
28 employed 50 to 99
18 employed 100 to 199
16 employed 200 to 499
 3 employed 500 or more.

Thus, 76 percent of the plants employed fewer than 100 persons. The average work force for all migrating plants was 80.

Reasons for relocation were obtained from the principals of 85 of the migrating plants. The five main categories reported were: space, taxes, labor, consolidation, and miscellaneous. For 49 plants, the reasons given were within one of the above five categories exclusively:

Space problems, 34 plants (69%)
   Need for additional space, 11 plants
   Cost of industrial space in New York City, 4 plants
   Need for horizontal space, 3 plants
   Combined space problems, 16 plants
Consolidations,[3] *12 plants* (25%)
Miscellaneous, 3 plants (6%)
   City business climate, 1 plant
   Personal convenience of owner, 1 plant
   Harrassment by regulatory agencies, 1 plant

The other 36 plants cited multiple reasons. Space was cited in 30 migrations, taxes in 22, miscellaneous in 20, labor in 7, and consolidation in 6.

Thus, space problems contributed to 30 migrations in addition to being the single determining factor in 34 migrations; of the 85 plants for which reasons were obtained, 64 cited space problems, i.e., 75 percent of the total interviewed.

Since the data in the report were not classified by "jobs lost" versus "reason for moving," let us perform the approximate calculations below in order to obtain a crude indication of the number of jobs lost due to space problems.

Space problems as the exclusive reason for moving: 34 out of 85 plants questioned gave "space problems" as the exclusive reason for moving out of New York City. Assume the same proportion holds true for all 153 migrant plants. Thus 12,206 × 34/85 = 4,900 lost jobs attributable to space problems alone.

Space problems as one of two or more reasons for moving: 30 out of 85 plants questioned cited "space problems" as one of two or more reasons for moving out of New York City. Again, let us assume the same proportion holds true for

---

3. *Note:* Some "consolidations" could be regarded as additional "space" reasons: to be conservative, however, they will not be so regarded here.

all 153 migrant plants. Thus, 12,206 X 30/85 = 4,300 jobs attributable to space problems in combination with other factors.

As a rough indication of the magnitude of the space problem, we can therefore infer that a total of some 9,200 jobs in 1965 were lost to New York City due, in some degree at least, to space problems (i.e., 75% of all jobs lost).

Rough cross-check: Data contained in the report for 47 firms were analyzed (see Table 11). It was found that only 3 firms moved into smaller space than that occupied in New York City, and 4 firms moved into plants with the same amount of space. The remaining 40 firms (85%) expanded by amounts ranging from 8.5 to 540 percent. The expansion in space incurred by all 47 firms taken together amounted to 62 percent. This tends to corroborate our inference above that a substantial number of jobs were lost because of space problems in New York City.

Table 11
Space and Employment Before and After 1965 Migration From NYC for 47 Manufacturing Plants—Data Extracted From the Burstein Report

NYC space (sq. feet)	New space (sq. feet)	New space as % of old space	No. of employees while in NYC	Space/employee while in NYC
36,000	65,000	180%	60	600
4,500	23,000	510	20	225
33,000	78,000	240	50	660
100,000	165,000	165	200	500
5,000	10,000	200	15	333
2,500	6,000	240	7	357
4,000	14,000	350	28	143
10,000	75,000	750	50	200
7,300	11,000	150	30	243
1,000	3,640	360	10	100
22,000	35,000	160	90	244
20,000	30,000	150	100	200
60,000	60,000	0	100	600
35,000	38,000	110	40	875
116,000	200,000	170	185	625
15,000	35,000	230	135	111
70,000	140,000	200	260	270
6,000	12,000	200	13	460
4,000	9,000	230	15	266
16,000	20,000	125	35	457
40,000	60,000	150	31	129

Table 11 (Cont.)

NYC space (sq. feet)	New space (sq. feet)	New space as % of old space	No. of employees while in NYC	Space/employee while in NYC
50,000	124,000	250	252	199
3,000	10,000	330	15	200
20,000	25,000	125	35	572
18,000	28,500	160	143	126
18,000	25,000	140	51	353
30,000	60,000	200	177	170
6,000	21,000	350	10	600
10,000	50,000	500	43	233
25,000	59,200	240	62	403
12,000	25,000	210	20	600
24,000	20,000	(85)	32	750
11,000	25,000	230	24	460
5,000	20,000	400	30	167
2,000	2,000	0	6	333
3,500	10,000	285	35	100
12,000	12,000	0	50	240
20,000	30,000	150	30	667
18,000	22,000	120	35	515
78,000	53,000	(70)	220	355
2,500	16,000	640	10	250
9,000	9,000	0	5	180
174,000	125,000	(70)	225	773
6,000	20,000	330	20	300
6,000	11,000	185	63	95
8,500	10,000	120	10	850
20,000	35,000	175	83	240
1,198,800	1,938,000			

Causes of Manufacturing Decline in New York City

The 12,206 jobs lost in 1965 through migration of 153 manufacturing plants are masked in the employment totals presented in Table 10 and Figure 1. Manufacturing employment actually increased by 5,000 between 1964 and 1966, although it decreased by 15,000 between 1965 and 1967. The migration of plants is only one factor in the changing employment pattern in New York City. Some observations, drawn from Dr. Burstein's report, are given in the following paragraphs.

Within New York City's manufacturing complex, large numbers of small establishments are constantly started by individual entrepreneurs. As some of them merge, become bankrupt, discontinue, or migrate, others fill the void and repeat the process with a few succeeding and others failing. In recent years, however, this process has slowed down. The number of manufacturing units in the city decreased by about 4,000 between 1958 and 1965, and by about 1,000 between 1964 and 1965. Thus, although the city's manufacturing complex may not have grown smaller in terms of output, it is shrinking in terms of numbers of units, entrepreneurs, and jobs.

This decline can be ascribed to many causes stemming from national and local changes affecting the location of industry. The Burstein report stated: "The changes included the emergence of the South into the industrial age, the shift of the nation's center of population westward, the disparate rates of population growth in the city and nation, the rise of affluent new markets large enough to sustain additional industrial complexes, and technological changes which facilitate dispersal. All have combined to bring about redistribution of facilities and relocation from long-established manufacturing centers, of which New York City is the largest. . . .

"Thousands of communities throughout the nation have organized development agencies, and their emissaries have been besieging this city's manufacturers with offers of special inducements such as tax abatements, financing, cheap labor, cheap or free land, and construction to specifications. In many instances they have also undertaken to train a labor force to fit the needs of a particular manufacturing establishment. Many firms transferred their manufacturing operations from the city in order to gain the competitive advantages afforded by these special inducements.

"A series of local factors have also contributed their share to the dispersal of manufacturing industry. Land and rental costs have always been higher in this city of eight million people crowded in 320 square miles of space. The wage differentials between this city and other communities were formerly large enough to induce certain labor-intensive sectors of manufacturing industry to seek out locations with an abundant and cheap labor supply. In more recent years, some of the city's industrial space has become obsolescent, and large-scale urban renewal and civic improvement projects have taken land out of industrial use. Taxes, too, have been instrumental in raising the cost of operating in the city. . . .

"The relocation-pattern bears seeds of further erosion of the city's manufacturing complex. Many migrants, aware of the singular advantages accruing from a New York City location, cling to the city's periphery. The proliferation of industrial parks in the counties of Nassau and Suffolk in this state, and in nearby counties of New Jersey, and the New York City manufacturing plants streaming into them, are evidence enough. The new industrial concentrations in the surrounding areas are, however, generating and building up their own external economies and will in time become progressively less dependent on this city's. They will themselves, in turn, become magnets for attracting more plants now domiciled in this city. . . .

"There are large numbers of bankruptcies and dissolutions of manufacturing establishments occurring annually in the city. Changes in public taste and demand for particular products is one important reason and competition from other areas, domestic and foreign, is another. Diminution (or lack of growth) in local employment is also brought about by the fact that some manufacturing processes can be performed cheaply or more efficiently elsewhere as, for example, publishing and radio assembling. An investigation of these factors, correlated with the migratory movement, may lead to finding that this city's industrial mix is at fault and needs redirection.

"An increase in the rate of mechanization (automation), and improved techniques made possible by a better-educated and trained labor force, have raised productivity and output per employee, thus allowing for higher total output with fewer workers. There is one more factor which is entirely in the realm of speculation, for lack of any information about it; it is the exodus of middle-class people from the city. . . .

"It is hardly likely that New York City could have retained manufacturing plants wandering off in search of expanded or new markets. Nor could this city offer the kind of financial inducements provided by some southern and other communities in search of industry.

"The 1965 relocation-pattern demonstrates, however, that most plants were anxious to retain their hold on this city's markets and external economies. If measures were taken to neutralize some of the advantages derived from relocation, it might be possible to slow down (even if not stop altogether) the outflow of plants. . . ."

Reducing Delay in Court Operations

INTRODUCTION

It is a basic precept of our society that justice should not be administered with one eye on the clock and the other on the checkbook. It is often the fact, however, that justice in the United States is rationed because of the limited resources at its disposal and the inefficient way in which they are used. At the same time justice may be effectively denied because of inordinate delays between arrest and final disposition. The techniques of modern management technology can help to achieve the most efficient use of the available resources, within the limits of procedures designed to ensure the due administration of justice.

In this analytic example,[1] the Task Force has focused its attention on the processing of defendants through a court, with special emphasis on the reduction of delay. Various solutions in the problem of delay have been suggested by judges, lawyers, and court administrators. Whether or not any of these solutions would indeed reduce delay can only be determined after they have been put into effect. In order to make preliminary tests of some alternatives without disrupting the operating courts, the Task Force examined the feasibility of using computer simulation techniques for experimenting with various modifications in the criminal court processing system. The judicial decision-making process was not a subject of this study.

Because court systems in the nation differ in organization and procedure, no single model will serve to represent them all. The approach taken was to test the feasibility of simulating one of these systems, namely the system for processing felony defendants in the District of Columbia. The steps followed were:
1. describing in detail the organization and structure of the court system for processing felony defendants
2. analyzing the available data on felony defendants in the U.S. District Court for the District of Columbia to determine the distribution of total time to disposition, time intervals between major events in the system, potential areas of delay and possible causes

---

1. The example is drawn from Chapter 4 of the Task Force Report, *Science and Technology,* prepared by the Institute for Defense Analyses for the President's Commission on Law Enforcement and Administration of Justice, published in 1967 by the U.S. Government Printing Office, Washington, D.C.

It deals with the processing of felonies in the District of Columbia and illustrates the application of a systems approach to a complex problem and the use of computer simulation techniques.

3. developing a computer simulation of the processing of felony defendants in the District of Columbia trial court system which:
   a) operated like that observed in the data (i.e., to produce the average time intervals between steps in the process similar to those observed in the data);
   b) could be manipulated to investigate possible organizational or procedural changes in the system and to measure their impact on delay and on resource requirements.

The District of Columbia Court System for Processing Felonies

The various steps and the associated resources for processing felony defendants in the District of Columbia court system are shown in simplified form in Figure 1. The first step is presentment, which occurs before a judge of the Court of General Sessions (the general jurisdiction court of first instance of the District of Columbia) or the U.S. Commissioner. Both are available for presentment and preliminary hearing in felony cases. Presentment is often preceded by a review or screening of the case by an assistant U.S. attorney, Court of General Sessions Division. He determines whether to reduce the felony charge to a misdemeanor, to terminate the case ("no papering"), or to proceed with prosecution.

The case is next processed in the office of the U.S. attorney, Grand Jury Unit. It is screened again and calendared for presentation to the grand jury. The grand jury votes on indictment if there is concurrence of 12 or more of the jurors. Thereafter, the indictment is signed by the foreman and by the U.S. attorney and returned (generally on Monday) in open court.

Arraignment is the next step. It is generally a perfunctory proceeding in which the accused appears, is advised of the formal charge and enters a plea—usually not guilty. At about this time the case is assigned to an assistant U.S. attorney who will probably handle it until final disposition, and a defense counsel is appointed by the court for a defendant who cannot afford counsel.

Following arraignment, trial preparation proceeds, motions are filed and heard, the case is placed on a calendar and, finally, progresses to trial. Only about 30 percent of the 1965 dispositions resulted in a trial; approximately 55 percent pleaded guilty to the offense charged or to a lesser offense prior to or during trial. The remaining 15 percent of the defendants were dismissed.

Time Delay in Processing Felonies

The time delay problem was approached by analyzing in detail the data on 1,550 felony defendants whose cases commenced by filing of indictment or information in the U.S. District Court for the District of Columbia in 1965. The time periods that these defendants were in the court system were compared with the timetable developed by the Commission's Administration of Justice Task Force. That

Figure 1
System for Processing Felony Defendants

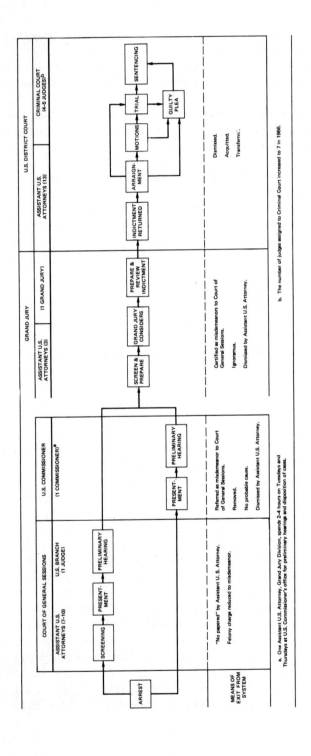

a. One Assistant U.S. Attorney, Grand Jury Division, spends 2–4 hours on Tuesdays and Thursdays at U.S. Commissioner's office for preliminary hearings and disposition of cases.

b. The number of judges assigned to Criminal Court increased to 7 in 1966.

timetable proposes that the period from arrest to trial of felony cases be not more than 4 months, with a maximum of 14 days from initial appearance to formal charge. The circled numbers in Figure 2 show a further breakdown of maximum time periods between the various steps in the processing of felony cases as recommended by the commission. Also included in this figure are the 50th percentile (median), 80th percentile, and 100th percentile (maximum) times observed in the 1965 District of Columbia data. Measured against the recommended timetable and evaluated in terms of best estimates of actual court and attorney time spent on consideration of a case, it can be seen that appreciable delays do exist. For example, 50 percent of the defendants who waived preliminary hearing had an elapsed time between presentment and return of indictment of greater than 42 days, whereas 20 percent had an elapsed time greater than 72 days. The maximum observed time was 269 days. From arraignment to guilty plea the elapsed time for 50 percent of the defendants exceeded 64 days, whereas 20 percent had elapsed time greater than 124 days, with a maximum observed time of 463 days. The timetable recommends a maximum of 63 days between arraignment and trial.

In summary, one-half of the defendants who pleaded guilty or were dismissed were in the court system longer than 4 months, 20 percent longer than 7 months. The defendants who went to trial took a median time of over 5 months from initial appearance to conviction or acquittal, 20 percent longer than 9 months. Contrary to generally held beliefs, motions were not the main cause of delays. Only one-half of the defendants filed one or more motions; however, one-half of these were filed more than 40 days after arraignment.

Experienced lawyers have pointed out that most of the steps in the actual processing of felony defendants require very little actual court time. The initial hearing for a defendant takes only a few minutes; a preliminary hearing usually takes between 15 and 30 minutes; a grand jury can hear, deliberate, and vote on the average case in less than 30 minutes; arraignment takes a few minutes; most motions can be heard in 10 minutes. A guilty plea requires as much court time as it takes a defendant to answer a dozen questions. The court time spent on a defendant who pleads guilty (approximately one-half of the felony defendants) probably totals less than 1 hour, yet in the District of Columbia the median time from initial appearance to disposition is 4 months. The data indicated that one-third of the time was spent waiting for return of the grand jury indictment. After arraignment on the indictment, additional time is required for the preparation of the necessary papers. But for the typical case, the actual time devoted to this process is a few days at the most, not weeks or months.

Computer Simulation of Processing Felony Cases

To study the impact of alternative methods of alleviating the delay in the processing of felony cases, the Task Force developed a computer simulation of the

Figure 2
Number of Days Between Steps in Processing of Felony Defendants—1965

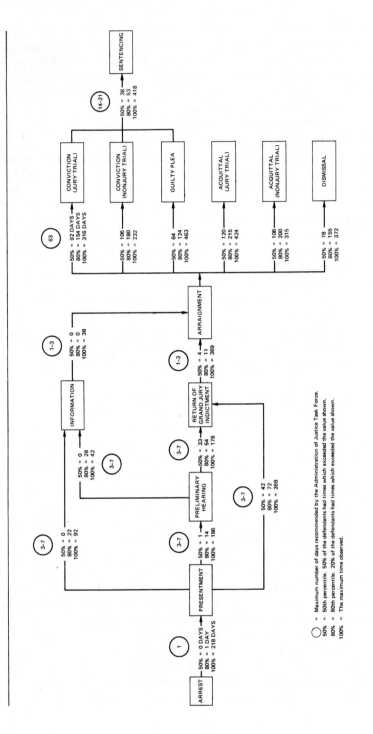

court processing activity. The simulation permitted experimentation with the court operating procedures with no disruption to the actual court operation. To make best use of the limited time available, an established simulation language was selected, IBM's General Purpose Systems Simulator (GPSS). The language, designed primarily for simulating industrial production processes, proved quite adequte to handle the court process.

The resulting model was called COURTSIM. Figure 3 is a flow diagram of the process as it existed in the District of Columbia Court system. The circles represent processing units or "milestones" in the processing of a felon. For example, the circle labeled PRS represents the Court of General Sessions, U.S. Branch, where the defendant makes his first appearance before the courts. The circle labeled USC represents the U.S. Commissioner, where defandants can also be presented. The arrows from one circle to another indicate the possible paths that the processing of a defendant may take; for example, from ARR (arrested) he may be presented to the U.S. Commissioner or his case may be discussed with the DAA (an assistant U.S. attorney, General Sessions) for possible presentment at PRS. Finally, the squares represent possible locations in the process where a defendant may exit from the system due to a dismissal, reduction of the charge to a misdemeanor, "no paper," etc.

The numbers on the arrows represent the percentage of defendants from each processing unit which take the indicated path. These percentages were estimated from the data and by staff members of the President's Commission on Crime in the District of Columbia.

COURTSIM was used to simulate the flow of the 1965 felony defendants through the District of Columbia court system. As the model is presently designed it does not handle the small percentage of cases that require exceptionally long times between events in the system; these could be incorporated into a later version.

The results of several of the simulation runs are presented in Table 1 with a summary of a few of the more important time intervals starting from presentment of the defendant. The first row presents the median times from the 1965 District of Columbia data. The last row presents the recommended timetable of the Administration of Justice Task Force. The other rows contain the times generated by computer simulation runs.

The second row is a time summary of the simulation using the conditions in 1965. In 1965, one grand jury was sitting and an average of five district court judges were assigned to the criminal part of the court. Under these conditions, the simulation reflected the actual court operation. In both there was an average time of approximately 6 weeks between initial presentment and the return of an indictment, and an average of at least 13 weeks from arraignment to beginning of trial. The close correspondence between the actual and the simulated times suggests that the model is a valid representation of actual operations.

Figure 3
Flow Diagram of Court Simulation

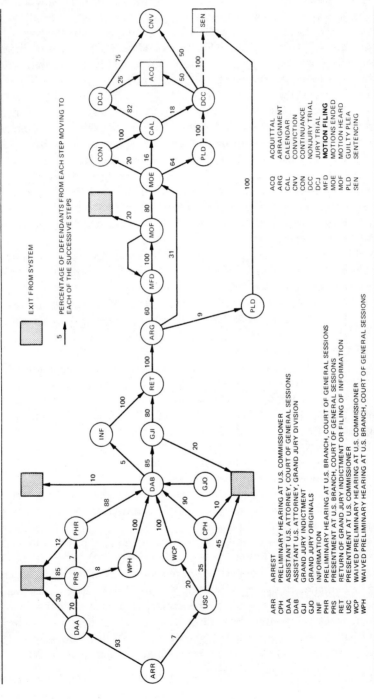

EXIT FROM SYSTEM

5 → PERCENTAGE OF DEFENDANTS FROM EACH STEP MOVING TO EACH OF THE SUCCESSIVE STEPS

ACQ   ACQUITTAL
ARG   ARRAIGNMENT
CAL   CALENDAR
CNV   CONVICTION
CON   CONTINUANCE
DCC   NONJURY TRIAL
DCJ   JURY TRIAL
MFD   **MOTION FILING**
MOE   MOTIONS ENDED
MOF   MOTION HEARD
PLD   GUILTY PLEA
SEN   SENTENCING

ARR   ARREST
CPH   PRELIMINARY HEARING AT U.S. COMMISSIONER
DAA   ASSISTANT U.S. ATTORNEY, COURT OF GENERAL SESSIONS
DAB   ASSISTANT U.S. ATTORNEY, GRAND JURY DIVISION
GJI   GRAND JURY INDICTMENT
GJO   GRAND JURY ORIGINALS
INF   INFORMATION
PHR   PRELIMINARY HEARING AT U.S. BRANCH, COURT OF GENERAL SESSIONS
PRS   PRESENTMENT AT U.S. BRANCH, COURT OF GENERAL SESSIONS
RET   RETURN OF GRAND JURY INDICTMENT OR FILING OF INFORMATION
USC   PRESENTMENT AT U.S. COMMISSIONER
WCP   WAIVED PRELIMINARY HEARING AT U.S. COMMISSIONER
WPH   WAIVED PRELIMINARY HEARING AT U.S. BRANCH, COURT OF GENERAL SESSIONS

Table 1
Representative Felony Processing Times in Days

COURTSIM run		Presentment to					
	Return of indictment	Arraignment	Guilty plea	Dismissal	End of motions[a]	Ready for trial	Time in queue at grand jury unit
1965 data (median days)............	40	53	107	134	148	[c]167	?
1965 basic[d]...............................	47	54	116	122	152	160	36
1965 basic with grand jury queue eliminated	16	24	90	102	–	127	8
1965 basic with grand jury queue eliminated and zero transit times....	6	8	48	14	–	56	<1
1965 basic with all cases processed through U.S. Commissioner	61	64	131	140	–	164	45
1965 basic with rule 87; guilty pleas at 30 percent........................	38	40	68	58	70	88	31
1965 basic with rule 87; eliminated queue at grand jury..................	7	9	37	27	39	57	<1
Administration of Justice Task Force model timetable (maximum days)...	14	17	80	–	[b]55	80	–

a. Cases with at least one motion.
b. First motion decided.
c. To trial date.
d. The mean number of days is used in rows 2–7.

The simulation indicated that most of the time prior to arraignment was spent in the Grand Jury Unit awaiting return of indictment (5 out of 7 weeks). By simulating the system with a second grand jury sitting part of the time, the time spent in the Grand Jury Unit was reduced from 5 weeks to less than 1 week, resulting in a time of approximately 2 weeks from initial presentment to return of the indictment. This is shown in line 3 of Table 1. Thus, it appears that for a cost of probably less than $50,000 per year for the additional grand jury and associated support resources, the delay from presentment to return of indictment could be reduced by 70 percent. The total time until the defendant is ready for trial would be reduced from 160 days to 127 days.

The fourth row gives a lower bound on the average times if, in addition, all transit times were eliminated, i.e., as soon as one processing stage finishes with a defendant, he proceeds immediately to the next and waits only if the next processor is unavailable because of weekends or he is busy. If such a condition had existed in the District of Columbia courts in 1965, a defendant would take an average of approximately 2 months after presentment to be ready for trial. Comparing these times with that of the last row (the Administration of Justice Task Force recommended maximums), one can see that the timetable appears to be reasonable.

An organizational change was next examined, namely the preliminary processing of all defendants was done by the U.S. commissioner (instead of by both the commissioner and the U.S. Branch, Court of General Sessions). The results of this run (row 5) indicate that the workload of the commissioner was not excessive and that the time from presentment to return of indictment was not significantly increased.

An additional example of the use of the simulation is in examination of the possible consequences of changes in defendants' behavior resulting from changes in court procedure. Accordingly, the inputs to COURTSIM were modified to reflect some of these procedural changes and potential effects. These modifications include such factors as (1) a decreased number of defendants pleading guilty, a possible result of the Bail Reform and the Criminal Justice Acts (2) a delay in the entry of a guilty plea and (3) the amendment of rule 87.[2] In addition, the current calendaring system was incorporated under which cases are scheduled for trial with priorities given to jailed defendants and old cases. The 1965 work load, in terms of number of defendants and their general flow through the system, was used in these simulations. Rows 6 and 7 show the average times with one grand jury sitting regularly and with an additional grand jury sitting when necessary (to keep the average waiting time in the grand jury unit under 1 day). The results of these runs of the simulation indicate that by

2. Amended rule 87 of the U.S. District Court for the District of Columbia which became effective October 1966 provides that motions are to be filed within 10 days of arraignment and heard the second Friday thereafter; arraignments are to be held the second Friday after the return of the indictment.

requiring motions to be filed and heard according to rule 87 and increasing the grand jury resources, the average time from arraignment to ready for trial was halved from 15 weeks (Row 2) to approximately 7 (Row 7). The average time from initial presentment to ready for trial was 57 days or approximately 2 months. Adding 1 month for the time from ready for trial to sentencing suggests that, on the average, the overall processing times would be less than 3 months as opposed to the 6 months (160 days plus 1 month). The time to guilty plea or dismissal is similarly reduced significantly, as is shown in those columns.

The above analyses indicate that the timetable of the Administration of Justice Task Force is practical. More generally, simulation appears to be an effective tool for examining reallocation of existing resources or efficient allocation of additional resources.

A critical factor in the above simulation runs was the required versus the available processing times associated with each step of the process (e.g., indictment, trial). Since data were generally not available, these times had to be estimated from direct observations and from officers of the court. The estimates appear to be reasonably accurate for the simulation to reflect the actual system in all the stages of the process up to trial. Although the estimates of the required and available trial times were based on the best available data, they may be optimistic. Further analysis of available and required trial times is required in order to investigate the sensitivity of the results to deviations in the estimated times used in the above simulations.

An important immeasurable factor not accounted for is the effect of changes in processing on the actions of defendants and court officials. The human in the system adapts to his environment and any changes made to it. The model assumes the various changes made will not affect the feedback process. For this reason, before any changes can be seriously proposed, the results of the simulation must first be thoroughly analyzed and discussed in detail with the court officers.

The major conclusion of this study is that simulation of the court process is indeed feasible and, properly used, can be a useful tool to the administrator of a court. The development and use of such a tool requires the collection of the relevant data. The simulation techniques developed here should be extended to several large urban areas as pilot studies with federal support to determine their applicability to other court systems and to develop them in further detail.

Part Four: Appendix

Appendix: Notes on Planning, Analysis, and Evaluation

INTRODUCTION

Much semantic confusion surrounds the terms planning, analysis, and evaluation. As used in these notes,[1] we define them as follows:

- Planning is a process by which an organization decides upon its objectives, selects the methods to attain these objectives, and subsequently measures the degree to which its objectives have been achieved.
- Analysis is the systematic organization of information in useful ways, usually to assist in making better-informed decisions by examining the probable costs and consequences of alternative courses of action. Analysis has a role in the planning process to assist in the selection of objectives and the methods to attain them.
- Evaluation is that particular kind of analysis which examines the degree to which current programs are achieving desired results.

Planning, analysis, and evaluation are all concerned with the use of information to help make better-informed decisions.

Exhibit 1 depicts the planning cycle. The cycle begins with analysis—the identification of needs and issues, selection of objectives, choice among alternative strategies, and design of an operating approach (program) to solve the problem or achieve the objective.

During the operation of the program, an evaluation study is performed. How well is the program achieving its objectives? All may be well, in which case the program continues to operate as before. Or, minor modifications may be required to make the program more effective. Or, fresh problems may be identified requiring further analysis.

The remaining sections of these notes discuss various aspects of the above process in more detail: types of analysis; steps in analysis; goals and objectives; program measures.

1. These brief notes were prepared by Graeme M. Taylor on behalf of the Department of Administration, State of Alaska, as an introduction for staff analysts to some techniques of analysis. This paper was written as part of a contract to recommend improved planning and budgeting practices for the State of Alaska.

Exhibit 1
The Planning Cycle

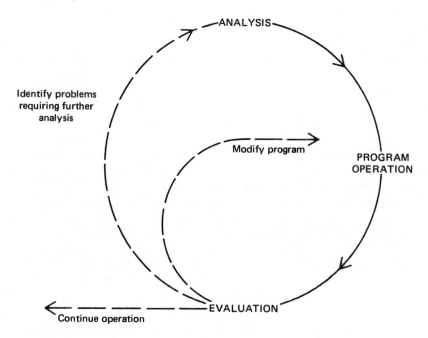

TYPES OF ANALYSIS

As used here, analysis is defined as: The systematic organization of information in useful ways, usually to assist in making better-informed decisions by examining the probable costs and consequences of alternative courses of action.

This is a very broad definition. There are many different kinds of analysis, or different ways in which the analytic approach can be put to use. A few of the variety of ways to think about analysis are discussed below.

Subject Matter

The subject of analysis can vary. For example, analysis can be performed on methods of improving operating efficiency or achieving economies. This is usually referred to as *management analysis*. Typical topics would include: "Lease Versus Buy" decisions; "Contract Versus In-House" decisions; work simplification ("Systems and Procedures") analysis, and the like. On the other hand, analysis can be applied to finding solutions to program problems—issues that affect the kind, level, and quality of service provided to the people. This would be referred to as *program analysis,* in which the effectiveness of the programs in achieving public objectives is the paramount consideration.

Program Analysis and Program Evaluation

The term "program analysis" is usually reserved for analysis of situations in which choices have to be made about the future. When the analytic approach is applied retrospectively to help answer questions such as: "To what degree has the program been successful in accomplishing its objectives?" this is usually referred to as *program evaluation.*

Different Techniques

Much has been written about cost-effectiveness analysis, cost-benefit analysis, systems analysis, etc. These terms are in fact jargon expressions which in reality describe quite simple notions.

A cost-effectiveness analysis attempts to provide answers to the following sort of question: For a fixed level of achievement of an objective, what are the costs of each alternative method of achieving that level ("equal-effectiveness" analysis)? For a fixed cost, what level of achievement of the objective can each alternative produce ("equal-cost analysis")?

A cost-benefit analysis goes one step further. It attempts to answer this question: How much benefit to the people of the state will be produced by a certain expenditure on each of a number of alternatives? (Either: How much benefit for a given cost? or How much will it cost to produce a given benefit?)

Here is an example. Suppose analysis of a manpower training program for Aleuts is being performed. One objective might be: "to reduce percent unemployment among Aleuts." Alternatives might include institutional training programs, on-the-job training programs, day-release training programs, etc. The analyst could attempt to estimate the percent reduction in unemployment that might be expected if $1 million were spent on a particular alternative (cost-effectiveness). On the other hand, if he attempted to estimate how much additional income would be earned by graduates of the $1 million training program, then he would be performing a cost-benefit analysis.

The term "systems analysis" does not really describe a different kind of analysis—hopefully, an analyst uses a "systems approach" when performing any analysis. A systems approach, or a systems view, merely implies that the analysis consciously attempts to view the problem in broad terms, recognizing the obvious fact that programs are very often interrelated. An action taken in one program will probably cause repercussions in another program. For example, increasing state trooper funds to solve more crimes and produce more arrests will probably require increased effort on the part of the district attorneys, the courts, and corrections. (It may also increase welfare costs for those families who are no longer supported on criminal earnings!)

Another commonly used analytic technique is "marginal analysis." Often, public decision makers are faced with requests to increase funding for a program by, say, 10 percent, or reduce funding by 15 percent. (This type of decision is encountered far more frequently than decisions to launch totally new programs or completely abolish existing programs.) In such cases, the analyst must estimate how much *additional* effectiveness or benefit will be produced by the extra funds, or how much effectiveness or benefit will *decrease* with the lower funding level. This is marginal analysis.

In virtually all program areas, effectiveness does not increase or decrease in a "linear" fashion with respect to expenditures. Suppose program expenditures are currently $100,000 and effectiveness is 100 (measured on some scale). It would seem that each $1,000 is producing 1 unit of effectiveness. But this does not mean that an additional $100,000 spent on the program will produce an additional 100 units of effectiveness: It may produce only 75 units or it may produce 120 units. Discovering these cost-effectiveness relationships is one of the tasks of marginal analysis.

STEPS IN ANALYSIS

A general summary of analytic steps is depicted in Exhibit 2. More detail on each is provided below:

Define Problem

What is the problem? The real issue, not the apparent or surface issue.

What caused the problem? How severe is it? Who is affected by it? Will the problem continue at present level, increase, or decrease?

What should be the scope of the analysis? In terms of (*a*) effort invested in the study (*b*) time horizon used (*c*) breadth of coverage of topics—narrow versus broad.

What systems and subsystems are involved? Can a systems view provide fresh insights on the problem?

Define Objectives

Objectives should be formulated in measurable terms (e.g., not "improve health" but rather "reduce the incidence of measles among teenagers").

Objectives should express what the agency, or the program is really trying to accomplish—not paraphrase a description of activities. What are the desired end results?

The analyst should recognize that it is not always possible to measure attainment of ultimate objectives, but substitutes can frequently be used. For example, it may not be possible to measure the reduction in pain and suffering

Exhibit 2
Steps in Analysis

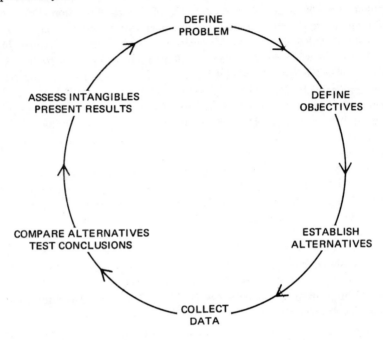

achieved by reducing highway accidents, but the analyst can estimate factors such as (*a*) number of lives saved (*b*) percent reduction in accidents by type and severity of accidents (*c*) reduction in number of hospital-days, etc.

One single objective will rarely suffice; most public programs have multiple objectives.

Establish Alternatives

Considerable creativity and imagination may be required to define practicable alternatives.

Initially, as many alternatives as possible should be generated—these should then be reduced to a manageable number of genuine, feasible alternatives for more intensive study.

"Constraints" should be explicitly recognized when screening alternatives—funding constraints, political constraints, technical constraints, manpower constraints, etc.

The analyst should remember that "do nothing" is always an alternative.

Collect Data

Data must be collected, or estimated, on the costs and consequences of each alternative.

There are many sources of data—information systems; previous plans, studies, and reports; other jurisdictions; surveys, samples, and questionnaires; pilot experiments; agency personnel's judgment, etc.

Data will often have to be projected, and estimates made.

It is crucial that the analyst carefully document the assumptions used and the basis on which data projections were made.

Compare Alternatives, Test Conclusions

Assess the relative costs and consequences of the alternatives.

Identify the "trade-offs" involved i.e., how much effectiveness or benefit will be produced or lost with different combinations of alternatives?

Identify the major uncertainties involved. How significantly do these uncertainties affect the desired outcomes?

Perform equal-cost, equal-effectiveness, and marginal analysis as appropriate.

Test conclusions: How do estimated costs and outcomes change if the assumptions are varied? What are the key assumptions and the most important variables? Can they be refined to produce more reliable information? Show ranges of outcomes rather than single points.

Formulate recommendations.

Assess Intangibles, Present Results

Identify major factors not previously weighed in the analysis (usually intangible or nonquantifiable factors).

Assess their impact on the recommendations. Rank the alternatives on the basis of the intangibles—pros and cons.

Reformulate recommendations.

Summarize highlights of the analysis and prepare briefing package to present to the decision makers. Include discussion of major uncertainties and assumptions.

Present and explain conclusions.

It must be pointed out that the above suggested analytic steps are very generalized. In practice, different analyses may follow quite different sequences. For example, the analyst must often begin by gathering data—in order to define the problem adequately.

To conclude this section on steps in analysis, the following precepts and rules of thumb are offered:

1. Analysis is only an attempt to gather information in a structured, systematic, ordered fashion. Analysis does not *make* decisions. Hopefully, good analysis can *permit* a decision maker to make better-informed, more rational choices. The result of an analysis is only one of many factors that may be considered in making a decision.

2. Analysis must be useful to the decision maker. This means that:
   a) The decision maker must decide what should and should not be analyzed; he must initially define the problem; it must be his objectives that are formulated and alternatives he believes practical that should be studied. The analyst can provide technical assistance, but the analysis must serve the needs of the decision maker. Therefore, the decision maker must be willing to spend time helping to define the study.
   b) The study must be completed on time, if it is to be of any use to the decision maker.
   c) The study should be appropriate to the problem. An elaborate, complex, sophisticated analysis is rarely required. The study should, as rapidly as possible, provide the information required to assess the choices confronting the decision maker.

3. Beware of hidden assumptions.

4. It is very easy to confuse means and ends; take care that the analysis is not self-serving—descriptions of what the program is doing should be differentiated from what the program should be accomplishing.

5. Ensure that the analysis documents (*a*) data sources, and (*b*) the basis for all estimtes (particularly projections).

6. Analysis can be "quick and dirty"—a rapid pulling together of information to solve an immediate problem—or it can result in a formal, written document that is addressed to a long-range problem. Both are useful.

7. Analysis is too important to be left to analysts. Operating managers must become involved if the analysis is to be of practical value.

8. Analysis should be designed to supplement the informed judgment of experienced administrators, not supplant it.

GOALS AND OBJECTIVES

The following definitions are suggested:

Aims: A generic term for all words used to describe the end purposes of government. Goals and objectives are individual kinds of aims.

Goals: The broadest aims of government, relatively timeless, normally not quantifiable, usually associated with the top level of a program budget structure.

Objectives: The specific aims of programs, similar to goals but not timeless or broad, capable of quantification; usually associated with lower levels of a program structure.

In the above definitions, goals and objectives are differentiated, though both have several characteristics in common. Table 1 describes these characteristics.

Table 1

Characteristics of Goals and Objectives

Goals	Objectives
1. Language and terminology consistent and clearly defined	1. Language and terminology consistent and clearly defined
2. End product oriented	2. End product oriented
3. Not measurable in quantifiable terms	3. Measurable in quantifiable terms
4. Not necessarily operational	4. Necessarily operational
5. Relates to program, not organizational or functional achievements	5. Relates to program, not organizational or functional achievements
6. Probably will cross departmental lines	6. May or may not cross departmental lines
7. Must be compatible with aims of higher jurisdiction	7. Must be compatible with other agency objectives and state goals.
8. Timeless	8. Shorter lived
9. Reflects problems endemic to most jurisdictions	9. Reflects current problems peculiar to the state
10. Broad truths	10. Specific aims
11. Identifies broad target population segment	11. Identifies specific target population segment
12. Developed by highest levels of government administration	12. Developed by program managers at the organizational level

PROGRAM MEASURES

Various measures exist which are helpful in providing a quantitative summary description of a program.

- – Program size indicators
- – Work-load measures
- – Output measures

    – Effectiveness measures

    – Benefit measures

The distinction among the above measures is not always precise. The following definitions may, however, be useful:

Program size indicator: A statistic which indicates the magnitude of program coverage or effort.

The most appropriate measure for a particular program will depend on the nature of the program. Some examples follow: number of classes; number of projects; number of inmates; number of people served in a particular target group; number of applicants.

Work-load measure: A statistic which indicates the volume of work to be done. For example, number of letters answere; number of applications processed; number of vaccinations given; number of court cases heard; number of inspections made.

Output measure: A statistic which indicates the volume of goods or services produced by a program. For example, number of graduates; board feet of timber harvested; number of successful rehabilitations; number of accidents prevented.

Effectiveness measure: A statistic which indicates degree of attainment of an objective. For example, percent reduction in unemployment; percent reduction in incidence of a disease; percent reduction in recidivism; percent reduction in traffic accidents.

Benefit measure: a measure of the value to society of attaining an objective. For example: increase in expected lifetime earnings as a result of having completed a training program; reduction in welfare costs.

In addition to the above program measures, two other types of measures are commonly used:

    – Input measures

    – Performance measures

Input measure: A measure of resources employed. For example, number of positions required for a program; cost; classroom space; amount of vaccine required.

Performance measure: A measure that relates work load or output to input; sometimes, a measure of operating efficiency. For example, number of cases successfully closed per officer; cost per patient-day; response time (e.g., time for an ambulance to reach an accident, or a fire-fighting team to reach a fire).